D1473958

TELLING HIS STORY:
POW #1000
THE BATAAN DEATH MARCH AND JAPANESE POW CAMPS

J.C. PARDUE

AND

JANIS PARDUE HILL, PH.D.

COMPILER AND EDITOR

LifeRich
PUBLISHING®

Copyright © 2022 J.C. Pardue and Janis Pardue Hill.

All rights reserved. No part of this book may be used or reproduced by any means, graphic, electronic, or mechanical, including photocopying, recording, taping or by any information storage retrieval system without the written permission of the author except in the case of brief quotations embodied in critical articles and reviews.

LifeRich Publishing is a registered trademark of
The Reader's Digest Association, Inc.

LifeRich Publishing books may be ordered through booksellers or by contacting:

LifeRich Publishing
1663 Liberty Drive
Bloomington, IN 47403
www.liferichpublishing.com
844-686-9607

Because of the dynamic nature of the Internet, any web addresses or links contained in this book may have changed since publication and may no longer be valid. The views expressed in this work are solely those of the author and do not necessarily reflect the views of the publisher, and the publisher hereby disclaims any responsibility for them.

Any people depicted in stock imagery provided by Getty Images are models, and such images are being used for illustrative purposes only. Certain stock imagery © Getty Images.

ISBN: 978-1-4897-4227-8 (sc)
ISBN: 978-1-4897-4228-5 (hc)
ISBN: 978-1-4897-4226-1 (e)

Library of Congress Control Number: 2022910531

Print information available on the last page.

LifeRich Publishing rev. date: 11/29/2022

CONTENTS

This work is dedicated to
my father, J.C. Pardue (POW #1000),
and all the patriot heroes who
marched and battled on Bataan in defense
of the ideals of the
United States of America.

I wish with all my heart I could tell my father and every other hero who marched on Bataan and walked with death for over two years just one more thing, just one more time— Thank you!

Thank you for, in the words of Hemingway, your "grace under pressure"! Unlike Hemingway, however, I do not think you accepted that in the end you would lose. And you did <u>not</u> lose! In your facing the enemy with perseverance and your belief and faith in God, *you won*!

PREFACE

Telling the story of the Bataan Death March demands two basic requirements: first, a dedication to committing to words a story of *atrocities beyond belief*, and second and simultaneously, a *cold detachment* from the details of the despicable torture and murder of American and Filipino soldiers on Bataan. Even when one has read and researched extensively the events leading up to the fall of Bataan, the horror hurts; the suffering evident in the photographs and in the words of survivors cuts to the bone. When one of the suffering soldiers is a father, husband, or brother, the ability to establish a conscious removal from the grisly reality presents an even greater undertaking. An enormous struggle, I have, nevertheless, determined to accomplish my goal and fulfill my last promise to my father— "to tell his story"—in his words—so that, now, even eighty years later, another voice from this tragic period in our history will be recorded for the descendants of this "Greatest Generation."

Also of importance, however, is the goal of informing many young people, and some not so young, of the details of one of the darkest periods in American history.

Although the Bataan Death March is recognized by historians as one of the most horrific examples of mistreatment of prisoners and blatant war crimes in the history of our country and the world, I have been amazed for years that a large number of individuals—educated individuals—do not know what happened in the Philippines after the bombing of Pearl Harbor (1941) and in the POW slave camps in Japan after the infamous march of death (1942-1945). Did history textbook editors and/or teachers not consider it important to include all aspects of the war? When Hollywood produced a movie about Bataan with no mention of the suffering and deaths of thousands of American patriots on a death march, was it because they did not know what happened? It is certainly not because of a lack of books published by some of the actual survivors. Many are still in print. The story must not be ignored or forgotten.

Regardless of the cause, myriad American patriots understand the necessity of preserving our nation's history and honoring our forefathers, whether they be a grandmother or an uncle or a great-grandfather. As a daughter of a World War II veteran, what stands as most important to me, at this point in time, is that eighty years ago, in a country on the other side of the world, men fought, suffered, and died for their country; and I want their children, grandchildren, and great- grandchildren to know that a great many Americans, across generations, appreciate that sacrifice. That is the cornerstone of my goal: to tell the story of the Bataan Death March—one more time—through the eyes of my father—and to celebrate—eighty years later—the courage and strength of an extraordinary group of American patriots.

A secondary goal of this work is to raise the consciousness of this frequently overlooked period in World War II. Ever the lifelong learner and researcher, I discovered as I recorded my father's words that I wanted to know more about the people, places, and the events he mentioned in his writing. Similarly, I hope the readers will be inspired as well to begin, or to continue, the study of these battles, islands, and other aspects of this epic world conflict that produced this remarkable group of American patriots, that group known as "The Greatest Generation." As I have acquired a greater understanding of my dad's experience from the words handwritten by my dad many years ago, so do I want the readers of this work to know and understand what it was like for the valiant, persevering soldiers of Bataan.

—Janis Pardue Hill, PhD

ACKNOWLEDGMENTS

I must thank, first, my husband—my rock—Charles Hill, who from the beginning to the end has "believed in my belief" that my father's story should be told. His encouragement and interest inspired me, as did the support of both my children, Trey and Amy, who loved their grandfather dearly. Amy, thank you for being always willing to give me your opinion on word choice, sentence structure, and assorted English "stuff"; and Trey, thank you for your assistance any time I needed help with a photo or resource.

I also appreciate the encouragement from a myriad of friends and other family members but must mention, specifically, my Aunt Joye, who shared pictures and memories, and my first cousin "once removed," Annette Daniels, who has become the friend my dad said I had to meet and get to know. Thank you, all!

Finally, and most importantly, I thank my Lord for directing me along the path that He thought I should take. Like my father, I believe that only through faith, with Bible in hand, can we make it through the challenges of life.

AMERICAN P.O.W.
#1000

ONE

Introduction: Heroes and Ordinary Men

W ithin the yellowed, crumbling pages of my father's "Former POW Medical History," which until the recording of his story I had never pored over, I discovered an incredibly revealing response to the final question on the last page of the document—a response I believe to be indicative of not only his character but also the character of many of the thousands of men who suffered through the Bataan Death March and subsequent years in Japanese POW camps. The question and my father's response are as follows:

Question:

In Spite Of The Many Negative Aspects Of Your POW Status, Were There Any Positive Aspects To Your Experience? YES X NO _____

If Yes, Please Specify: Greater faith in God; the greatness of America (U.S.A.); individual courage & dedication is of the utmost importance in the cause of Freedom; never over-react to desperate circumstances, even under hostile captive conditions. (See Appendix 7)

In awe that anyone who had experienced what I had read on the previous pages (i.e., beatings, physical torture, psychological torture, intimidation, brainwashing) could find positive aspects, besides just "survival," I sat, amazed. When I revisited the list of positive aspects, however, I understood: these were the characteristics I had always observed in my father. He was that man of great faith, courage, and dedication to the cause of freedom listed in that response. Perhaps, I thought, he would have been that man without the Bataan experience. I doubt, however, those values would have been embedded so deeply and have been so much a part of who he was.

For years I did not know my father was an American hero. I never suspected that the quiet, kind, and gentle man who loved learning and who made it his goal to teach me to read and write to one hundred before I entered school had faced evil in its cruelest and ugliest forms: tyranny and lust for power at all costs. Not until my teen years would I learn that he was one of the thousands who endured not only the infamous "trek" known as the Bataan Death March but also two and a half years at the hands of the brutal, seemingly soulless Japanese guards: first as a prisoner of war and later as a slave in one of the Japanese factories. Typical of the World War II soldiers who now bear the label "The Greatest Generation," this ordinary man possessed humility of a sort often characteristic of men who fought in that war. These greatest of men fought with courage to overcome the foes that threatened their country, not seeking glory, not interested in the fame. They fought for one reason: love of a country founded on freedom and defense of the way of life they cherished.

Like many other survivors of the Bataan Death March, my father never said or acted like he was a hero; in fact, the one time I remember that I told him he was my hero, he choked up instantly—he seemed to gasp. Likewise, he never said he was not at some points scared. He did what he had to do to survive and to overcome the threat to the country and society for which he fought. Numerous survivors wrote of their experiences, horrific as they were, when they returned; and even though the account of one survivor often mirrored the accounts of his buddies, each must be considered from the perspective of the unique individual's story. *Each soldier's story is his or her own.*

My father's story reflects the personal strengths of all the men who marched up the Bataan peninsula—bravery, perseverance, selflessness—but it also reflects more when considered from the viewpoint of his personal beliefs, talents, and aspirations. That is the reward readers receive from reading and/or hearing the chronicles of these ordinary individuals placed in extraordinary circumstances that they never imagined they would experience. Like innumerable others, he enlisted prior to the United States' entry into World War II, hoping to improve his life after his service as well as to assist his family back home. I did not learn until late in my adulthood that my dad sent a generous portion of his checks back home to help provide for his parents and siblings. These men were humble, and they were generous. Very often, they are viewed as personifications of courage; but they possessed many other admirable traits as well, and these are the traits that leap from the pages of their stories.

An artistic spirit, my dad was blessed with a myriad of talents, from drawing to building a house for his family shortly after he left the service. As a child, I thought my daddy could do anything; as an adult, I learned he could—well, almost anything. He was very much a "many-sided" man who wanted to learn, to build and to create, and at the same time, provide for his young family. Upon returning to civilian life, my father enrolled in college on the G.I. Bill, the ticket to a return to normalcy for thousands of young veterans; and in a few years he made another march, this time down the aisle to receive his diploma. I was six years old at the time and vaguely remember the event, though its significance was lost on me at that point in my life. What elation that young man must have felt! I know this because my sister and I grew up understanding that we would go to college and graduate, not that the notion was pounded into our brains; rather, it was a goal we seemed to imbibe from our parents, with Daddy the guiding force behind our future higher education goals.

My father wrote prolifically about his experiences when he returned from the war. Most of his writing he kept private for many years, but after I learned the details of his war-time experience, I knew without asking why he kept those ruminations to himself for such a time. This was a man, like thousands of others, who had been beaten, imprisoned, and physically and psychologically tortured. I believe strongly that he used that time writing to reflect and to scrutinize that part of his life; as a deeply spiritual person, he sought understanding into one of the most atrocious examples of "man's inhumanity to man." Now, as a retired professor of English and Curriculum Studies, I understand the benefits of putting on paper ideas that are more than often too difficult to articulate. My dad employed personal journaling long before the classroom teachers learned how beneficial it could be for both students and adults. If he had not, he may not have survived what must have been many post-traumatic days and nights.

Daddy reflected and wrote, wrote and reflected, and then, as so often happens, life got in the way; and he put away his work, with the goal of one day publishing his work becoming less important. During this time, he visited schools when invited to share his story and was always willing to talk to young people one- on-one. Both of my children interviewed him as part of their social studies projects as did other students and friends. He was also active in ex-POW groups and was instrumental in the coordination of the fiftieth anniversary of the fall of Bataan at Barksdale Air Force Base in Bossier City, Louisiana. About a hundred miles from our home, Barksdale, ironically, was the base at which he began his military career and where he met an extraordinarily knowledgeable, caring counselor and a huge advocate for ex-POWs, Ms. Naline Salone. Daddy thought this lady was the absolute best adviser and counselor ever, and she was—a lady totally committed to taking care of the needs of veterans and ex-POWs.

Thus, the years went by; and when my dad's eyesight began to fail, it became clear to me, as I am sure it was to my dad, that he was not going to be able to complete his task of a complete compilation and publishing of his writings. Perhaps, deep down, the reflecting and journaling had fulfilled the need to confront head-on an experience so prominent in his life's journey—to address it, to learn from it, and then to leave it behind. I never asked him that; writing is a personal journey. However, when I saw the many pages (some handwritten on loose-leaf paper and some typed in revised format) I knew I could not let those pages continue to deteriorate in folders and boxes. "Daddy," I told him, "I'll put your writings together for you. I want to do that!"

He did not object and eagerly shared with me numerous details of his time as an American soldier.[1] What a blessed time that was, me with my laptop, asking and listening, and Daddy answering, and at times, seemingly straining to dig a memory out! I would not trade those times for any treasure on earth. And these were the days when I began to realize, truly and completely, what the soldiers of World War II endured to defeat the tyrannies that threatened not only the United States but also the entire world. My understanding increased tenfold as I sat down to those pages written so many years ago in my dear father's handwriting. Some of the passages had been revised and typed; but for the most part, this book comes from the written word, on the yellowed pages from a legal pad, flaking and crumbling at the edges.[2] How priceless these treasured pages are to me now! In fact, these fragile pages store a gold mine of memories and events that I, like many baby boomers, want recorded for my children and their children and their children.

Our young people need to know that eighty years ago, in a land half a world away from their home country, ordinary men and women accomplished extraordinary deeds in the name of liberty and love of country. Unknown to them at the time, they were destined to become participants in one of the most horrifying walks of all time, a walk so shockingly evil it was soon labeled a death march.

That walk, or march, transformed them in ways they never anticipated and certainly never imagined. Many, needless to say, bore scars, both physical and psychological, for the remainder of their lives. Because they had witnessed and suffered the brutality of the evil existing in some men, they returned home different from the men who had enlisted to fight years earlier, living with the memories of the torture, the executions of fellow soldiers, and the other horrors, but fighting to recover and live useful, productive lives in most cases.

Myriad accounts have been recorded of the difficulties the returning soldiers faced; but for the most part, they faced those ghastly memories just as they had faced the soulless Japanese guards: stoic, loyal to their fellow soldiers, and determined to survive, if possible. If not possible, then they were determined to fight to the end, if necessary. Of most consequence, however, is the positive effect on many of their lives when they returned, not that all the scars were gone or would ever disappear completely. However, the stature of the men they became overshadowed the scars left by the experience. Capturing this stature is an integral part of my core focus.

The following narratives comprise my father's collection of writings from his many journals and other essays over several decades. They cover both his entry into the United States Army Air Corps (which would in 1949 become the United States Air Force) and his experiences in, and after, World War II: the battle to hold Bataan; the surrender of Bataan; the horrifying, at times gruesome, experiences on the Death March; in the POW camps; as a slave laborer in Japan, and as a survivor determined to live a Christian life as a husband, father, son, brother, brother-in-law, uncle, and friend. *Most significantly, within these narratives, my father tells the story of his treasured Bible that he carried with him on his journey, its loss on three different occasions in the Philippines, and its miraculous recovery every single time.*

Like my dad, I believe that God had a hand in ensuring that Bible made it back home with him.

I believe also that my beloved father, like thousands of others who made that fateful journey to the Philippines, never thought he would be a firsthand observer of "evil in its most appalling form." Sadly, he was.

From his personal writings and interviews, this is his story.

—Janis Pardue Hill, PhD

AMERICAN P.O.W.
#1000

TWO

Enlistment and Preparation for War

L ike many other young men who graduated from high school during the Great Depression, I enlisted in the United States Army Air Corps seeking an opportunity to acquire skills that would lead to a successful career. I signed up on October 20, 1939, although my official entry is dated April 15, 1940. The first of thirteen children, I was born on October 25, 1917, to a cotton farmer and his wife in Union Parish, a northern parish in Louisiana. Of the thirteen children, eleven survived to adulthood; and all the boys served their country—four in World War II and one in Vietnam. My siblings and I grew up in a church-going family and were taught to respect our parents and teachers. We learned through observation of our parents and through following their examples that hard work pays off.

The Depression affected my family just as it affected all of our family and neighbors in North Louisiana. Although farmers were not devastated in the way farmers were in nearby Oklahoma, Kansas, and the other Dust Bowl states, Louisiana farmers were also affected by the national economic despair. The price of a pound of cotton dropped to just pennies, which forced my father and other cotton farmers to plant gardens, instead of cotton, in an effort to feed their families. Thus, we never went hungry, but times were hard; and like most Americans during the 30s, we lived simply and had few luxuries.

My parents were not wealthy, but they provided a home, clothing, and food; and they were well respected in the community. Most importantly, they instilled in their children a love of God. Both my parents worked hard, and all of us were expected to help, in the fields and inside our home. From them, my siblings and I learned to be honest, trustworthy, and loyal. My mother was the hardest working woman I have ever known. Because modern conveniences had not yet been invented, she did not have an automatic washer, dryer, or dishwasher. Despite that, she cooked three meals a day while at the same time devoting time to churning our butter, cooking our meals, working in the garden, canning vegetables, and caring for her children.

I remember one of my sisters, Ernestine, telling me that as a child she wondered why our mother churned butter when we had plenty. As an adult, she understood: it was an opportunity to sit down and rest. Our mama was also an accomplished seamstress, and she embroidered beautifully. My oldest daughter treasures a beautiful set of pillowcases my mother created for her after she was born. I don't ever remember Mama complain of being tired. She was a beautiful woman devoted to her family. Five years after I returned from the war, she passed away from cancer. I am so thankful I made it home before we lost her.

I graduated from high school as valedictorian. An engaged student, I loved school and learning. In those days, in the middle of a nationwide depression, most schools offered a basic curriculum of the 3Rs—reading, writing, and arithmetic; there were few options. Still, those students who paid attention and worked hard acquired the skills necessary to go further after graduation. Because of the G.I. Bill, I was able to enroll in college after the war and graduated with a degree in accounting with a minor in English.

When I enlisted at Barksdale Air Force Base in Bossier City, Louisiana, the United States was not at war although the sounds of war could be heard from across the Atlantic. Still, I enjoyed the training and the new environment in a big city where I could visit museums and experience a culture I had missed out on during my high school days in a rural area. I easily adjusted and began to enjoy my new surroundings, not knowing that in a couple of years I would be a prisoner of war in the jungles of a faraway country.

Suddenly, the stateside, enjoyable life style came to a halt. I never expected to be thrown into the center of a world war even though we had all heard for months the rumor that "war was coming." I do believe, however, that because of my upbringing, I was prepared, just as many of my fellow soldiers were prepared. There were some who said the demands of growing up in the Great Depression prepared my generation for what we would face on the battlefield. I was accustomed to hard work in the fields, sweating in the sultry heat of Louisiana; and when tools needed repair, my father taught us how to take them apart and put them back together so they would work. The idea of replacing them with new ones was never considered. Although I did not realize it at the time, these lessons in self-sufficiency and hard work served me well both in the Philippine jungles and in the steel factories of Japan.

At the time of my enlistment, Barksdale, which consisted of 2200 acres, was the largest base in the country, and that was where I trained for five or six months. It was at Barksdale that the 27th Bomb Group was organized. Constituted on December 22, 1939, (as the 27th Bombardment Group), it was activated on February 1, 1940. Altogether, I trained at three bases: Barksdale in Louisiana, Scott Field in Illinois, and Hunter Field in Savannah, Georgia.

In October of 1940, the 27th Group was sent to Savannah to open a new air base, Hunter Field. During that time, we performed the enormous task of carving a landing strip out of the dusty soil of Georgia. It was a job, but we did it. By July 4, 1941, the field was ready for the opening day, which was an "open" day for civilians to visit and take a ride through the base. It was evident to all that the visitors were amazed that an

Army air field had arisen so quickly within their state. We, as the "builders" of the air base, were equally amazed as well as quite proud of our endeavors.

After July 4, the 17th (my squadron), the 16th, and the 91st Squadrons of the 27th Group began training in preparation for the upcoming maneuvers, which were scheduled for the fall. It was a busy time as we worked on the assignment of becoming expert, first-class soldiers. The consensus was that it was during this time the 27th Group, through their training and cooperative labor, became a cohesive unit with members looking eagerly toward the maneuvers. Unknown to us at the time, the 27th Group would become known as an extraordinary unit in the defense of the Philippines in spite of the considerable number of adversities we would face.

The 17th, my squadron, was the first of the squadrons to leave Hunter Field, heading on August 18 for Shreveport and our first introduction to war maneuvers. We were sent to the Shreveport Municipal Airport where it was our assignment to stage a one-squadron war. This proved to be quite a task, as we flew for both the Red and the Blue armies until the 3rd Squadron joined us. It was a new experience for many of us, but, generally, most agreed the activity went fairly well with only a few stories, and at times calamities, to share later after we completed the exercises.

The most dramatic incident was the plane that lost an engine and landed in the Red River, which flows between Shreveport and Bossier City. The pilot survived and came out of the river with an interesting tale to tell. Another was the encounter another plane had with six high-power lines, blacking out a portion of the city's population and prompting a complaint from the power company. The most famous event of those first maneuvers, though, occurred when the 17th bombed its own cavalry. Their excuse was that it was difficult to distinguish which side a soldier is on when he is on both sides, the chief danger when you are in a one-squadron war.

All in all, it was said that the one-squadron maneuvers taught many lessons to the enlisted men and their superiors. At any rate, we had gotten our feet wet with the early maneuvers in Shreveport and were ready to leave for the famed Louisiana Maneuvers. Now that was something to see! The 17th Squadron was ready; at least, we thought we were. Looking back, we realized we actually had no idea what we would be facing on a lonely peninsula in the Pacific Ocean.

The Louisiana Maneuvers

When soldiers from all over the country were being transported to the Louisiana Maneuvers, the whole country looked like a revolutionary army coming in. The highways were loaded with truck after truck filled with soldiers headed to the maneuvers. The woods were full of soldiers. They were camped all over the western side of the state, from Shreveport in the north to Lake Charles in the south. We lived in tents—thousands of tents stretching for miles—and you could not imagine the line of trucks. Other maneuvers were held in the Carolinas and Tennessee, but the Louisiana Maneuvers were the largest at that time with nearly five hundred thousand soldiers called to the state to prepare for combat.

I was sent to the southwestern corner of Louisiana near Lake Charles for my part in the maneuvers, and like everyone sent to this area, my first memory is of "mud"—huge clumps of mud I carried around with me on my boots for days. The hurricane that hit South Louisiana about a week before the maneuvers began added even more swamp and marshy land to the area. Being a Louisiana boy, I was accustomed to the rain that often saturated our state, but camping and participating in war games on rain-drenched terrain added another dimension to the maneuvers. It was a busy time with the expected bloopers and successes. At the end of our time in these war games, however, we were praised for our record, especially since we learned later that the 17th, the 16th, and the 15th Squadrons flew many more missions than the other groups stationed with us.

All of us sent to the Louisiana Maneuvers had no idea that the maneuvers would go down in history as the most famous war games the United States military had ever conducted. Also unknown to us at the time was the fact that the Louisiana Maneuvers were, in one sense, the training ground for a few young officers who would become four- and five-star generals before World War II was over: George Patton, Dwight D. Eisenhower, and Omar Bradley were only three of the men there who would later be known as leaders and heroes of the United States during World War II. We heard Louisiana was chosen because the terrain on the Louisiana-Texas border, from northwest Louisiana near Shreveport to southwest Louisiana near Lake Charles, consisted of the perfect training terrain: dense forests with thick undergrowth, red hills, swamps, and rivers—a rough terrain, in other words. In the jungles of the Philippines, we appreciated that training.

General George C. Marshall, we learned later, was the primary force behind the war games in the United States. When General Marshall was named chief of staff, he had inherited troops that could not have survived combat in a world war of the sort he thought might occur, and he knew they had to be readied for combat. That is the reason he fought for permission to hold maneuvers in the United States. He said in 1941, defending the need for the maneuvers, "I want the mistakes [made] down in Louisiana, not over in Europe, and the only way to do this thing is to try it out, and if it doesn't work, find out what we need to make it work."[3]

I've been asked if there was a sense among the young soldiers that these massive maneuvers were in preparation for a war, and I can't say for sure there was. I don't know that there were not soldiers who may have thought that, though, because we were all aware of the war in Europe. I just didn't hear anyone talking about the United States preparing for war. You just trained. You trained in case of war, but you didn't actually talk about it. After the Louisiana Maneuvers, we went back to Savannah. My friend Goss had a red Oldsmobile convertible—that was "it" in those days. I thought I was somebody, and Goss did too! Goss and I went from Lake Charles to Bernice (in Union Parish) and then to Savannah.

When we arrived in Savannah, things settled down into a routine—at least, for about a week. Then a rumor surfaced that we were being sent to the Philippines. The "Philippines"! That was the first response for nearly everyone! The rumor brought about much confusion. Prior to that, we had no idea where we might be sent, with most of us not giving a lot of thought to it. Then we heard it was said "we were so good that they were going to send us (the 27th) to the Philippines." A complimentary assessment of the 27th, it was an appraisal which members of the group felt great pride in, but at the same time, the news brought about varied responses from members of the 27th Group.

The assignment pleased many of the soldiers because to most young GIs, the Philippine Islands were like a resort—where the "East meets the West." There was a spirit of anticipation, an opportunity to see the Orient. It was an outpost, some said. At that point no one dwelled too much on the possibility of war. One soldier I talked with had been in the Philippines for about six years; but another young soldier, F. W., worked to get a pass to go back to Fort Worth, and he did. He didn't come back.

Upon hearing the news, most of us didn't really give too much thought about military action at that time because, generally, we did not know the details of what the Japanese had been doing over there; and we didn't know what President Roosevelt knew or was doing. We did talk about our orders, which we were told was to open a new air base (Neilson Field) although there were already two fields in the Philippines— Nichols Field and Clark Field.

AMERICAN P.O.W.
#1000

THREE

Luxury Liner to the Far East

A fter the Louisiana Maneuvers in 1941, it was said that General Kruger remarked: "The 27th Bomb Group is the best tactical air force in the country." And then, they selected the 27th Bomb Group to be sent to the Philippines to defend the islands. The 15th Squadron, however, which was a squadron of the 27th Group, had been on loan and was training paratroopers in Fort Benning, Georgia. Reports were that General George S. Patton notified President Roosevelt that the 15th was needed to train paratroopers in Fort Benning, Georgia and that he was unable to release them for other purposes. As a result, the 16th Squadron, the 17th Squadron, the 27th Headquarters Squadron, and a material squadron were split for the formation of the 91st Squadron to complete the unit to go to the Philippine Islands. These were the squadrons comprising the 27th Bombardment Group which (after many days of packing) left Savannah, Georgia, for San Francisco, California, the port of embarkation. The date was October 19, 1941. It seemed much had changed as we said farewell to Savannah and boarded the troop train.

As I boarded one of the five troop trains that would transport the 27th across the nation, essentially from the East Coast to the West Coast, my thoughts traveled to my family back home in Louisiana. I pondered briefly about what they might be doing at that particular moment since a day on a farm was always filled with chores and labors necessary to keep the family fed. When I took my seat for the long ride across many states, I also wondered when I would see them again.

The five-day trip on the train was not a relaxed one; the train was crowded, and the food usually consisted of cold sandwiches if we were able to get food at all. I was eager to get the train ride behind us, but I eventually settled down and attempted to enjoy the scenery moving past my window seat: from the plains and the desert to hills and mountains— America rolled past the windows of our train as we made the trip from the east coast in Georgia to California on the west coast. Like many of my squadron, I had never seen these places before, so I was not bored. At last, we reached our destination: San Francisco, California, our last stop on US soil.

Angel Island

After arrival in Frisco, we headed to Angel Island, which was officially named Angel Island Immigration Station. I had heard of Angel Island before I arrived there and did know that it had been where immigrants from the Far East had been processed from around 1910 to 1940. That was about all I knew. For the 27th, Angel Island was the place we received a round of vaccinations against all the diseases prevalent in a tropical climate, and there were many. I wondered briefly how effective these vaccinations would be. Although I had no specific knowledge of the many diseases prevalent in the tropics, I suspected they did not guarantee 100 percent protection. The Army Air Corps mandated them, however, so I lined up with everyone else. Hopefully, they would help some at the least.

During this period when I was on Angel Island, the enormity of the journey facing me at this point in my life became prominent in my mind, and I began to give a great deal of thought about the course of events most certain to follow. I recognized that something was needed that would give me the great strength I would need to finish this journey. I speculated that it would take years of long endurance and that many deeds would have to be performed while in other lands if I were to pass successfully through the dangerous straits. It would be some time before I could once again return safely to America. While completing those final preparations on Angel Island, I became acutely aware of this and began to directly confront the desperate circumstances we very likely would be facing.

About a year before this time, I had obtained a small compact Bible (pocket size). It was approximately four and three-fourths inches by seven and one-fourth inches, and it was about five-eighths inches thick. I had selected that particular Bible because of the black leather cover with the zipper closing, and because it was the King James Version with a reference and concordance. Before we left Angel Island, a fresh thought came to me: I said to myself, "I'm going to begin reading the Bible throughout, starting at the beginning with the book of Genesis and reading from cover to cover until I finish with the book of Revelation." On many occasions in the past, I had heard, and it also had been related to me by biblical scholars and ministers of the gospel, that the information given in the Bible provides the answers to all of man's questions, a solution to all of man's problems, and contains, as well, the accurate set of directions to guide all the people in the world. The answers are timeless and are appropriate for any generation of problems.

With these thoughts in mind, I recognized and accepted that the entire needs for man's wisdom was available to me. This was within my grasp; with this little book I would have the necessary knowledge and wisdom at my fingertips in the near future. Thus, I started reading within the beginning context of the literature and began "feeling about" for the needs of understanding. I came to believe that the Bible does, indeed, offer divine insight to all the things that may be of interest to mortal man. This was the way I found it.

The Bible and its information would help me resolve and clarify the position where I stood and give me strength to endure any unfamiliar, challenging situations which my soldier friends and I might encounter. In these words of Truth, I found what I would call the map to the future routes and options that all people will seek to travel in this world. Therefore, I decided that it certainly could project a great light on the vast circumstances spreading before me in the times ahead.

During the voyage across the Pacific, I spent much time reading and studying my Bible, and I continued my search and reflection into the middle of March of the next year—1942. Therefore, this first reading was finished in the early years of the great conflict. Altogether, it took me about six months to read the material—the wisdom—inspiringly presented to me in the Bible. After I completed my goal of reading from Genesis to Revelation, one of *the most* important truths I learned is that the mustard seed of faith can move a mountain of any size. Faith is the golden passport that one must secure before traveling in search of knowledge, wisdom, and truth. I have taken this truth with me throughout my life, and it has served me well.

All Aboard

After our tasks were completed on Angel Island, we headed to the ferry boats, which carried us to the ship that would transport us to the Philippine Islands. The rumor we had heard weeks ago upon our return to Savannah from the Louisiana Maneuvers was now a reality. I looked at the size of the ship toward which the ferry was headed, thinking about the voyage ahead and once again about my family at home and what my sisters and brothers would think about my travel arrangements. The future was a blur at this point; but like many, I think, I couldn't help but feel a sense of excitement and pride in my fellow soldiers.

On November 1, 1941, the 27th Bombardment Group boarded the luxury ship, the USS *President Coolidge*, for our voyage to the Far East. For a great number of us, the ship we were boarding offered extremely luxurious accommodations for American soldier boys, most of whom had seldom been out of their home state. I was one of those "boys," but here I was with members of my squadron in San Francisco Harbor boarding the largest ship we had ever seen. We did not know it as we walked up the gangplank, but the trip across the Pacific would be in sharp contrast to the tents of the Louisiana Maneuvers, and the muddy swamps of Louisiana became a memory as we sailed under the Golden Gate Bridge. I took one or two last looks at my homeland before the ship glided into the Pacific Ocean; and, once again, I wondered when I would return.

The sadness at leaving my country was soon overtaken by the luxury of the ship's surroundings, even though the enlisted men were housed below in tier bunks with the staterooms being reserved for the officers. The "mess"—the food—was the highlight of the trip and not at all what we normally received in the mess halls on base. Throughout the entire voyage, we dined in the evening on foods such as steaks, prime rib, salmon, and squabs, as well as assorted vegetables and desserts. There was also an orchestra at every meal. The ship offered luxuries not usually enjoyed by enlisted soldiers: swimming pools, badminton courts, and deck tennis. In the evenings there were movies that were always packed as well as recreational activities like boxing, swimming, and badminton and deck tennis set up by a "recreation committee." The accommodations on the USS *Coolidge* definitely surpassed those of the troop train.

In an interview of three other former POW survivors and myself for a local newspaper article in 1967, one of my friends also remembered the luxuries of the voyage:

> We really traveled in style on that ship, first class all the way with orchestra music at every meal, delicious food, three swimming pools, badminton courts, and deck tennis. We often said they were just fattening us up for the kill. How true those words became later. . . . We went from a life of plenty, a life of complacency right into a war. It was a terrible change.[4]

Ironically, in only a few months, unknown to us at the time, the meals in the Philippines would be vastly different, and at times, nonexistent. We did eat well on the *Coolidge*, however. On the Bataan Death March and in the camps, there were many times I thought about the food I left on the very fine plate that sat on the equally fine linen tablecloths covering the tables on the USS *Coolidge*. During those times, I would have been satisfied with just the crumbs.

The voyage to the Far East on the *Coolidge*, which was just one of the American big ships making trips to Manila, Philippines, at that time, was not the typical military journey. Although it was being employed by the military for military purposes during this period, we were free of many military restrictions. Surprisingly, we were allowed to wear civilian clothes and permitted to spend a great deal of our time as we liked. Some soaked up the sun while others read, wrote letters, or played cards; and everyone filled up their plates at mealtime. A voyage across the Pacific on a fast liner like the *President Coolidge* took about sixteen days. We traveled under the secret mission code name "PLUM," the word stamped on all our gear and bags. As passengers on the *Coolidge*, this operation named "PLUM" seemed more like a vacation than a military operation. But that would change.

The 27th Bombardment Group of the Army Air Corps arrived in Pearl Harbor on November 6, 1941, just a little over a month before the infamous surprise attack on December 7. At around 6:00 a.m., the USS *Coolidge* approached Diamond Head, an amazing sight, and then a couple of hours later slipped into the docks in Honolulu. Almost everybody had appeared on the deck early to get, in most cases, their first glimpse of Hawaii. We were all issued passes around eight thirty and hurried ashore to see as much as we could in a few hours since the ship was to set sail again at 2:00 p.m. Many of my soldier buddies quickly located the first bar, but Roy, my first cousin, and I walked around and took in the sights. Roy bought a bunch of bananas, which I enjoyed too. Like the typical first-timer, I was in awe of the beauty of the island, but I didn't buy any of the brightly colored shirts or leis. I suppose my upbringing during the Great Depression had left an imprint on my spending since I had always been taught to be frugal.

After the short stay, we headed back to the *Coolidge* and continued our voyage. As we watched Hawaii fade in the distance, the ship's communication system made an urgent request for everyone to return to large compartments below for instructions and lectures. First, our squadron commander, Captain Lowery, revealed that we would be traveling from Honolulu to Manila under observance of wartime precautions: full blackout of the ship's deck at night and no striking of matches at night. He also said, "The two battle cruisers you see are for escort on the remainder of the voyage. They have sea-plane scouts on their deck to scout the water ahead." One was the Army Transport *Winfield S. Scott*, and the other one was the USS *Louisville*, which was a heavy cruiser.

It appeared clear to me then that conflict in the Philippines was very likely a possibility. Another hint was the addition of physical activities in the mornings and lectures later on topics like dive bombing and strategies to employ in all sorts of situations. Most helpful were the lectures given during the blackout nights by several officers who had seen prior service in the Philippines. I found the insight they offered to us extremely valuable. They had been there, so they had firsthand knowledge of the weather, the terrain, and the people of the islands.

At last, we entered Manila Bay, and we got our first sight of Corregidor, the mountain fortress MacArthur would later make his headquarters, and Bataan Field, both of which were on the left of the ship as we sailed on toward the famed city of Manila. On first sight, for those of us who were making our initial trip to the Philippines, the beauty of the tropical islands was as magnetic as we had been told. It seemed as if we had been sent to a tropical Garden of Eden. At the same time, however, we also noticed small boats in the bay. We learned later they were searching for survivors of an interisland boat, *The Corregidor*, which had been blown up by a mine in the bay. This news brought home to me and others that the luxury voyage was coming to an end, and the reality of war seemed closer than ever before. The date was November 20, 1941, eighteen days before the Japanese Imperial Army devastated Pearl Harbor.

AMERICAN P.O.W.
#1000

FOUR

Welcome to the Philippines:
A Tropical Paradise and World War II

T he USS *Coolidge* was greeted with a rousing welcome, a flyover of two P-40 fighters as well as military songs from the Fort McKinley regimental band, both of which increased the enthusiasm each of us felt upon our long-awaited arrival in the Far East. There was also an official Army Boarding greeting party. The fanfare was impressive, but all the enlisted men on deck, standing or wandering around, were eager to get our orders and "get off the ship." That did not happen immediately, however, as the army moves at its own pace, a fact we should have learned over the last few months.

After hours had passed, we were told at last to disembark and to load onto trucks that took us down Dewey Boulevard to Fort William McKinley, our temporary base. The ride was only a nine- or ten-mile drive, but it gave us the opportunity to see a small part of Manila. Running along the line of trucks in some parts of the city were young Filipino boys who greeted us with the typical, "Hi, Joe." They were smiling and friendly but also hoping for a coin tossed down to them. When the trucks finally drove through the gates of the base, I was happy and grateful to see the enlisted men's quarters, which consisted of many rows of tents set up for us on the golf course, located in front of the officers' quarters—not the luxury of the *Coolidge* but they looked adequate.

Like everyone else, I was hot and tired and ready to get settled into our quarters, but before that, we were honored with yet another welcoming address. This one was from General Jonathan Wainwright, who delivered a speech that none of us perceived as too welcoming since he spent a great deal of his message on wearing proper uniforms at all times, specifically, a coat and tie. He later withdrew this order after one of the officers questioned the practicality of that for men living in tents on an island in the Pacific. My first day on the Philippine Islands had been a long one, even in a tropical paradise.

American Forces

Two additional units traveled with the 27th, the 48th Material Squadron (a maintenance group) and the 45th Ordnance Company (bomb specialists); and all three were scheduled to be sent to a new airfield at San Marcelino, located north of Bataan on the western coast of Luzon. Because the airfield was not complete at the time, a few men of the 27th were sent there, with most of the 27th remaining at Fort McKinley. Neither had our airplanes arrived yet. Recognized as the one combat-ready dive bomber unit in the Army Air Corps at the time, the 27th, ironically, was the one group without planes. We were told they would arrive as soon as they became available from the manufacturing assembly line and as soon as the dive bombers could be shipped to the Far East by sea transport. This was not the first time we would hear this promise. As a result, without our planes, the 27th was given physical duties such as building revetments as well as other assorted duties to keep us busy.

Almost as unsettling as the lack of planes was the news that the Japanese were already at Fort McKinley when we arrived, and they were quite visible. In fact, during the time we were at Fort McKinley, the communication and radio crews of the 17th Bomb Squadron at Nielson Field detected and observed Japanese combat planes daily in the vicinity of our military installations. (Neilson Field, located just south of Manila, was situated between the city and Fort McKinley.) Although the communication and radio crews used the opportunity to gather available information about the Japanese air and naval activities taking place, the Washington High Command saw no cause for alarm at that point, or so we were told.

I soon learned alarming validation of the reason for our participation as part of the intended large air power buildup in the Far East: the anticipation of military action by the Japanese. Although our leaders in Washington did not publicly acknowledge this possibility at the time, it became known that the powers in Washington had fully expected war in the Pacific, presuming, as well, that the Philippines would be caught up in it. And that was the reason the United States had begun in the late summer of 1941 to increase its forces in the Philippines as relations between the United States and Japan deteriorated. Besides the 27th Bombardment Group, the American forces also consisted of two other large Army Air Corps groups: one was the 19th Bombardment Group, a bomber group; the other, the 24th Pursuit Group, a fighter command unit.

After the arrival of the newly added groups, the American and Philippine forces consisted of approximately 125,000 troops, but only 30,000 were US Army soldiers. The others included the Philippine Scouts and the Philippine Army, which comprised the largest number of soldiers. Although the Philippine Army had the benefit of American leaders, they lacked the training of the American soldiers, and they were poorly equipped. Another prime example of that poorly prepared force buildup that lacked equipment was my group, the 27th Bombardment Group—hundreds of soldiers—but no planes.

Other action was taken, as well, one of the primary ones being the call of General Douglas MacArthur out of his retirement in the Philippines and back into active duty to lead the US forces stationed there. Prior to this, MacArthur was serving as the field marshal of the Philippine military forces. It was generally known that MacArthur believed in the possibilities of the Filipino armed services if they could be properly armed and trained. Not one to minimize his own ability, the confident MacArthur believed he could successfully defend the Philippines; he could get those forces ready. Time would prove, however, that the leaders and strategists in Washington, DC had waited too long to prepare the necessary forces to defend the Philippine Islands successfully and too long to supply them with the aircraft and weaponry necessary for a military operation of this size.

Few would argue that Douglas MacArthur was the obvious and most logical choice. A decorated officer, MacArthur's record in World War I was impressive, and he loved the Philippine Islands where he, his wife, and young son lived at the time he was called back into active service. We heard, also, that the general loved the Philippine people. As a famous general, Douglas MacArthur had both admirers and critics. When we heard that MacArthur had been named Commander of the United States Army Forces in the Far East, there was much discussion about our newly named commander. Many who knew his history of service in World War I greatly respected his valor and reputation, but there were also some who had heard that his ego was larger than his service record.

Nevertheless, General Douglas MacArthur assumed his new position, seemingly with the same bravado and confidence he had approached every other assignment throughout his life and career.

I have contemplated many times during the postwar years about whether or not MacArthur's great confidence was a negative or a positive, especially considering that he was just one of the US leaders who had not taken the threat of the Japanese Imperial Army as seriously as they should have. In fact, it began to appear to many of us that they had never fully accepted the possibility that a Japanese attack was approaching sooner than they anticipated. In fact, when MacArthur received the message from Secretary of War Henry L. Stimson that an attack from the Japanese was imminent, the rumor was that it was a shock to him since he had always believed the Japanese would not attack until the spring of 1942. We, the average soldiers, never heard why he held this belief, just that he firmly believed that would be the case. This time General MacArthur, the great hero of World War I, was wrong. I have often wondered what he must have thought when his theory was contradicted and what impact it truly made on him.

High Alert

When MacArthur received the alarming message from Secretary of War Stimson, he, without delay, informed Major General Lewis H. Brereton, the commander of the Far East Air Force (FEAF) in the Philippines. As another highly respected, experienced officer, Brereton knew what that meant, so he immediately put all his units on high alert. To us, that meant the days and nights were no longer as relaxed as they had been, and the arrival of the 27th Bombardment Group's planes became a central concern. We were told, again, that they were on the way. In addition, during the next few days, innumerable preparatory actions were taken, including placing all units on war alerts as well as intensification of patrols both in the air and on the ground. We now knew the Japanese were coming; we just weren't sure precisely when or where.

Then, on December 7, 1941 (December 8 in the Philippines), the Japanese forces attacked Pearl Harbor. It was a date that President Franklin D. Roosevelt described in his famous speech as "a date that [would] go down in infamy." (See Appendix 4) It was also an attack that shocked the nation and the world—such a cowardly act that many civilians in the United States forgot or failed to take much notice that the Japanese did not stop with Pearl Harbor. Instead, the Japanese continued their assault on American forces in the South Pacific. The Philippine Islands were at the top of their list, but they were only a part of their planned invasion and occupation.

MacArthur had been informed almost immediately of the Pearl Harbor attack, and by many accounts (which were passed down to us, the average soldiers) was as stunned as most Americans. Word and shock spread across the squadrons. It was unbelievable to everyone, an improbable event that in our minds could not have happened, but it did. Having left Pearl Harbor only a few weeks prior to the attack, I am sure I was not the only one who thought back to our brief stopover on our journey over on the *Coolidge*. The famed beauty of Hawaii we had enjoyed for a few hours inserted itself back into my mind. I wondered what it must look like now. That any other nation's armed forces could surprise and overpower the core of the United States Navy was the discussion among members of every group. Not only were the Japanese ahead of MacArthur's tentative schedule, but they were also extremely prepared for both the devious attack on Pearl Harbor and the attack a brief ten hours later on the American forces on Luzon, the largest island of the Philippines. The American forces were not prepared—on either island!

Reaction and Response

The lack of preparation in the Philippines resulted in a grueling and costly day for the Army Air Corps on December 8, 1941. Also costly was the hesitancy among the U. S. leaders to make astute, quick-thinking decisions after the shocking news of the Pearl Harbor attack. According to accounts learned through the years, the first action MacArthur took after being informed of the Pearl Harbor attack, the notification of Major General Lewis H. Brereton, was a wise one; but that didn't turn out to be true for every action taken and every decision made. Fortunately, Brereton had previously placed all his troops on high alert.

The events that followed MacArthur's message to Brereton were unusual to many who later investigated the happenings of that unfortunate day. Early on the morning of December 8, Brereton attempted to see MacArthur to request permission to take his B-17s and bomb Formosa, which was held by the Japanese and near the Philippines. For some reason (not clear even after the war was over), however, General MacArthur's chief of staff, Brigadier General Sutherland, refused to allow Brereton to speak directly to the general. He chose, instead, to relay the general's refusal through him. When Brereton tried again to get approval, Sutherland, once again, relayed a message from General MacArthur that he did not want to attack first. Approximately five hours later, MacArthur called Brereton, giving him the approval to attack Formosa. Unfortunately, it was too late since the Japanese planes by then had left Formosa and were in route to the US airfields.

The Japanese attack on the Philippines was a repeat of their attack on Pearl Harbor. That the American forces did not greet the Imperial Japanese Army pilots with bombs and other firepower must have been amazing to the Japanese airmen. Instead, caught off guard by a strange set of circumstances, the American fliers were, very literally, in the wrong place at the wrong time. Although the American officers and soldiers were aware that the Japanese planes were coming, they were caught completely by surprise.

The planes at Iba Field had just returned from a patrol and were coming in for a refueling when the Jap planes destroyed every one of them. Likewise, the pilots of the planes from Clark Field, who also had been patrolling most of the morning, had returned for refueling and for lunch. They too, with their planes lined up on the field, were as easy a target as they could have provided the enemy. By the time the pilots saw the sheer number of planes heading toward them, and a few were able to scramble for their cockpits, it was too late. In a short time, therefore, the Japanese executed disastrous attacks on Iba Field and then Clark Field.

Clark Field—its planes, hangars, buildings, and fuel tanks—was devastated. The aircraft losses, at Clark Field especially, were catastrophic: eighteen of the B-17s were lost or damaged severely, and over thirty P-40s were destroyed. In addition, the strikes destroyed the communication across the islands. Fortunately, Brereton had wisely sent half of the B-17s to Del Monte Plantation, located five hundred miles to the south; or all of them would have been at the mercy of the Japs. It was known later to us that Brereton had worried about a surprise attack.

At Fort McKinley, we correctly expected the fort would be the next target, so we began immediately to prepare. We dug foxholes, and we watched the skies for enemy planes, but the attack did not come during the hours of light. The attack came late in the night, sending every soldier out into the night to the sound of thunderous bombs. It was chaotic and terrifying; and from the air, if there had been light instead of the darkness, it must have looked like a wild fire drill being conducted by half-clothed soldiers scrambling to respond to another surprise attack. It seemed the Japanese knew when and where to strike to inflict the greatest number of deaths and destruction.

Confusion reigned on that fateful day and night, and it was more than the bizarre set of conditions and disorder that contributed to the defeat. The reality, according to the many experts (solders, analysts, and politicians) who later assessed the disasters at Clark and Iba, is that MacArthur and his indecision helped to set the stage for the tragic consequences suffered by the American forces. On the ground we heard both sides of the story, and neither is acceptable for the actions and performance of armed forces of a country considered a power on the world stage.

One group of soldiers clearly thought the blame for the devastation of the US forces belonged squarely on the American officers and their soldiers. Others gave them the benefit of the doubt, I suppose, would be the best way to explain their viewpoint, pointing out that the American planes had been in the air patrolling for the enemy planes without the knowledge that the Japanese planes were still on the ground on Formosa due to a heavy fog. There was an element of chance, some said, that when the Americans returned to their bases for refueling, the Japanese caught them with their planes on the ground.

Through the stories that circulated, we learned that MacArthur's actions highly inflamed the temper of Brereton, who believed the heavy bombers he commanded could have made a difference. Because General MacArthur, however, refused to give permission for an air war due to orders from Washington, the eighteen B-17 bombers remained on the ground and were destroyed by the Japanese planes. Many believed that if Brereton had been given permission to take his troops to Formosa and attack the Japanese first, those American planes would not have been parked like "sitting ducks" on the ground.

Obviously, MacArthur held on to Washington's orders that, in the event of military aggression by the Japanese Imperial Military Command, American defenses in the Far East were absolutely forbidden to fire on attackers to defend themselves until Congress declared a formal declaration of war. Thus, by the time Congress in Washington had made the formal declaration of war, the Japanese had shot up and destroyed about 90 percent of American planes parked along the runways in the Philippines. President Roosevelt had the authority, and MacArthur would not go against the wishes of his grand chief in the president's chair in Washington.

Washington and its bureaucrats, according to many soldiers, politicians, and historians, should also have shared the blame for the incredible December 8 defeat of the Americans and Filipinos in the Philippines. For months they had delayed the arming of the Philippine Islands with the necessary equipment and munitions, all during a period when the American leaders remained most concerned and committed to assisting the British against the Germans. This, obviously, to them took precedence over the Philippines, in spite of the fact that the powers in DC did realize that the Japan-United States relationship was deteriorating.

Japan wanted and needed the oil reserves in the South Pacific, and when Roosevelt placed embargoes on the oil, the stage was set for the aggression by the Japanese. As I learned after returning from the war through the many reports that became available, President Franklin D. Roosevelt firmly believed in his commitment of American forces and equipment to the British in their fight against the Germans; and the American soldiers in the South Pacific suffered because of that. This I believe.

Continued Attacks

As disastrous as the losses inflicted by the Japanese were on December 8, the destruction was not sufficient for the Imperial Japanese Forces, who did not cease their attacks. In the weeks that followed, we, the ground troops, continued to endure the bombing raids and strafing—day after day after day. In the beginning, the alarms prior to the attacks brought instant fear to all of us as we suspended whatever we were doing and dove into foxholes or behind the barriers constructed for protection. After a while, though, they became a commonplace event to be tolerated during the course of our day's work and, as a result, somewhat less frightening.

I guess we were becoming accustomed to the sounds and images of war—a sad commentary when I think back to the death and destruction that accompanied those many raids. Sometimes during a raid, a soldier (at times, a close buddy) was caught too far from a foxhole or protection and did not make it to safety. These were the images difficult to erase from one's mind as the raids continued. To see a fellow soldier's body ripped to pieces and scattered on the ground is not easily forgotten; it lives in your head for years.

With few planes left, the Americans depended on the few that remained after the attacks, including a few of the B-17s that had not been destroyed at Clark Field and were able to be repaired. It seemed there was always a plane to be patched up or parts to be replaced. The US forces continued to fight, but the Japanese Army had dealt a devastating blow to the American Air Corps. It was during these times we discussed once again the topic of our missing planes, which were supposed to have arrived weeks ago.

In addition, a large number of the 27th Group began receiving infantry training since it rapidly appeared we would soon need it, and many in my squadron had little or no experience with firearms. We were each issued old World War I 30-06 rifles that had been stored for years in Cosmoline, a thick grease used to protect weapons in storage. After we had removed the Cosmoline, we were instructed in both marksmanship and taking care of our rifles. Being a country boy familiar with hunting and firearms, I was not a novice in the use of rifles and shotguns. It did seem a little ironic though. When I entered the Air Corps, I did not expect to be infantry, but in a strange turn of events was in the process of becoming a foot soldier. For a moment, I missed the rows and rows of cotton that had to be picked on our farm, a backbreaking job. In my current situation, it didn't seem too bad anymore. That world seemed so distant that I wondered if I would ever get back to those fields of cotton.

Land Invasion

Thus, the days in December of 1941 passed, primarily by dodging bombs and strafing or by practicing our shooting skills. Ever present during our days, though, were the rumors and reports of the next stage of the Japanese campaign: the invasion of ground troops. Once again, we knew they were coming; we just were not certain when and where. The first drives, which occurred on December 10, two days after the devastation of our airfields on December 8, were two small invasions at Aparri and Vigan on the northern shore of Luzon. We learned later there were about four thousand Japanese troops in those invasions.

The second invasion, one day later, December 11, was on Legaspi, located on the far southwestern shore of the island. The Japanese obviously had a plan, which was to move through the Philippines from several directions and then take Manila. They were using these first invasions as preparatory, establishing air fields and getting ready for the main invasion, which would be a massive one. The Japs were easily successful as there was little resistance from the worn-down American forces, even as they anticipated the main invasion. We knew it would be soon, and it was.

On December 22, 1941, approximately eighty transports under the command of Japanese Lieutenant General Masaharu Homma landed on the southern end of Lingayen Gulf on the western coast of Luzon. Their goal was to fight their way down from the northern part of the island, through the mountains, to

Manila, located about 125 miles to the south. With that landing, the Imperial enemy had us outnumbered ten to one. Despite the difficulties, the American forces and the Philippine Scouts attempted to defend their ground and slowed the Japanese forces some on that first day. It did not help that most of the Filipino soldiers turned and ran as soon as the first shots were fired. Overall, however, the American forces and Philippine Scouts were not prepared in number or skill for Homma's Fourteenth Army, which numbered over forty thousand. At the end of the day, with permission from MacArthur, the American forces retreated behind the Agno River.

The second day was even more devastating for the American and Filipino forces, who were clearly inadequate to resist the number and the training of the Japanese forces. And it got worse the night of December 23 when the Japanese landed about ninety-five hundred troops on Lamon Bay, only sixty miles from Manila. At that point, MacArthur realized his forces that remained could not resist the assault from so many sides; thus, at the end of the day on December 24, he made the decision to retreat to the Bataan Peninsula.

The Retreat to Bataan Begins

Although we did not know it at the time, a retreat to Bataan, if necessary, had always been part of War Plan Orange, so this was the plan put into effect. The retreat of the North Luzon Forces and the South Luzon Forces, though it was not the intended outcome, was well organized. Wainwright and the other generals, wisely and strategically, employed maneuvers to slow the enemy as much as possible, thus allowing their troops to retreat. They dynamited bridges and erected as many barriers as they could. The Japanese invasion and subsequent defeat were decisive, but our leaders did accomplish the successful withdrawal of forces from the battlefield. MacArthur knew that he had to get his soldiers off Luzon before Manila fell.

As a result, verbal orders to head to the docks of Manila were given and passed from commander to commander wherever they were. Specifically, orders were for us to take whatever we could carry and get to the Manila docks. When my commander at Fort McKinley got word of the orders, he located trucks to take us straight to the docks. Others showed up in Manila on buses; some, in cars. For a while, it was wall-to-wall soldier, most without clear information as to where this mass of military personnel was going.

Fortunately, we beat the Japanese there although many of the men had been told they were right behind us. This, of course, ignited even more confusion and chaos, given the huge crowds of soldiers waiting on the docks for boats. Adding to the frenzied hectic environment were fires and explosions lighting up the night sky as our ammunition and supplies were destroyed to keep them out of the hands of the Japanese. The thought crossed my mind that this spectacle was not too much worse than the air raids at Fort McKinley. Later in the night, my squadron loaded onto an interisland steamer bound for Bataan. Maybe things would get better.

We boarded the Filipino interisland steamer at the

waterfront in Manila on Christmas Eve and floated all night in Manila Bay. Around daybreak, one of the colonels shouted, "Let's get off this thing before we get an air raid on this boat." Hearing that, we all jumped off into a few feet of water, not knowing what was ahead of us but expecting American airplanes to arrive later. Once again, those planes never came. *The 27th Bombardment Group is the only air force in history that fought as infantry.*

By December 25, the Japanese occupied most of the main island of Luzon; and on January 2, 1942, they entered the city of Manila and seized control. Unknown to us on December 24, as we voyaged on our interisland steamer to the Bataan Peninsula, General MacArthur had declared Manila an "open city." He did this, thinking that the Imperial Japanese Army would abide by international law. Instead, they destroyed the city that had been called the "Pearl of the Orient" because it was so beautiful, and they began immediately to commit horrific war crimes. What the barbaric Japanese soldiers did to the city and its citizens clearly revealed their hatred for the Filipinos as well as their ruthless cruelty. At the same time as his declaration, MacArthur also moved his headquarters to the island of Corregidor.

After the capture of Manila, the Imperial Japanese took control of the large stockpile of food supplies destined for American soldiers. The enemy, of course, was thrilled about the good things under their control; it must have been like a gold mine to them. However, they had a fight still as the entrance to Manila Bay was under blockade by the big guns on Corregidor and the mines in the bay. I have always thought that except the good Lord held the eyes of the Imperial Japanese forces and kept them glued to the large food supply in Manila, they could have bypassed the Philippines, which possibly could have had an impact on the progress of the forces fighting in other parts of the world. That was probably just wishful thinking on my part, thinking what a difference that food would have made to us on Bataan.

Some of my buddies and I discussed why the Japanese did not go back and finish what they started at Pearl Harbor, mainly taking the large oil supply tanks up on the mountain slopes or going and finishing off Australia. This would seem to have been no problem for the Japanese Navy since it was in control of about one-half of the Western Pacific, excluding Australia and some other small areas. It was said they attacked Australia sixty-four times but did not try to take it. Instead, the Japanese kept the planes of the regular air force in the air over the Philippines most of the time; day and night they made bombing raids over Bataan and Corregidor.

As it turned out, the decision of the Japanese to focus on the Philippines gave the Allied forces the opportunity to do everything possible to help the European theater, and it kept the supply lines moving. There were reports that the United States was shipping masses of supply ships and a huge percentage of the Air Corps to Great Britain and the Allies. We also heard that German U-boats sank around 240 of those ships. The assistance from the United States, however, made a significant difference to both the British and our other allies.

AMERICAN P.O.W.
#1000

FIVE

Christmas Day Arrival on Bataan

I t was Christmas Day, December 25, 1941, as we made it ashore from a Filipino interisland steamer. We landed at what we would later learn was Mariveles, on the southern shore of Bataan Peninsula. It was the dry season. I remember the smell of dust, the tropic air, and the crying of lizards in the trees, but my most vivid memory is the solitude—a stillness, a silence—that seemed to forecast a warning of future dangers. Noting that there was no one to greet us, I waded ashore from the interisland steamer with everyone else. My group of about 100 to 110 soldiers had all been on the same boat. I knew all those men. Roy, my first cousin who was in the Headquarters Squadron, landed at the same time. There were also some soldiers from the 16th Squadron and the 31st Infantry arriving as well.

We had no idea of our whereabouts as my platoon began marching up the dry hot road with only a prayer to keep us going. Most of the men in my group had not seen a bite of food for the past twenty-four hours, and we had no emergency rations. I did get one piece of chocolate candy from a box someone passed around. I was one of the lucky ones who had a "Christmas meal"; not everybody got a piece. We marched forward, each with a canteen of water and an Army Springfield rifle, which was the only standard equipment for all members of my squadron. The one exception was Sergeant Wallace, who was in possession of a Browning automatic rifle, the only fully automatic weapon in our unit. I also carried a .45 automatic pistol, but it was not fully automatic. Additionally, I carried one personal item in my field pack—my compact Bible consisting of the Old and New Testaments.

As I beheld the splendor of the tropic island beauty for the first time, I thought surely there must not have been such beauty displayed or duplicated elsewhere in nature. That was my first impression. I had heard the silvery waters surrounding the Philippine straits hosted a chain of seemingly endless rain-swept tropical islands with magnificent scenery. And now, even in the worst of circumstances, I understood the fascination with the beauty of the islands. Although I was hungry and thirsty, the scene would have called most first-timers to take a second look, especially those of us who had been brought up in rural America. I took one more look at the view along the bright coral shorelines and white beaches that offered such eye-catching beauty, and then I turned away. Maybe on another day there would be time. But not today, and not likely anytime soon, I thought.

Thus, starving and poorly equipped, the 17th Bomb Squadron Provisional Infantry was on the march up the peninsula on the National Highway, moving toward that inevitable confrontation with the Japanese Army located somewhere on the island of Luzon. On a map of the Bataan Peninsula (which is roughly thirty miles long and fifteen miles wide), the National Highway appears relatively straight; however, on foot it is a crooked road that follows the inlets of Manila Bay. Therefore, our Christmas Day trek was a scenic one, with Manila Bay on the east and Mount Bataan to our west. However, few were interested in the scenery that Christmas morning. We had one thing on our mind—food. We were looking for something to eat since it had been over twenty-four hours since we had eaten. We had not yet adjusted to functioning with only crumbs or scraps for our daily meals; that would come in the near future. We just thought we were hungry on this particular morning. We would soon find out what real hunger was.

As we left the landing strip and continued up the island toward the seaport town, the possibility of running into one of the stores and buying something to eat was prominent in all our minds. Unfortunately, every one of the stores in Mariveles was boarded up; six to eight to maybe ten stores were nailed shut. It looked like a deserted village; we did not see anybody. The residents had obviously abandoned the seaport town to escape the Japanese bombing flights. With no hopes of food, we headed on to Cabcaben, observing for the first time a close-up view of the rugged terrain we would be defending: mountains, dense jungle covered with vines and undergrowth, and bamboo trees along the gorges and streams.

During our march up the National Highway, I observed a bitter attitude from the members of a few of my group, most likely from our dire situation. We were eight thousand miles away from home, plagued with hunger, and equipped with antique rifles from World War I to fight a modern war. Having never been clearly and completely briefed on our mission in this foreign land, it seemed we were without a clear objective. Added to that, the air overhead throbbed with flights of fifty to one hundred planes at a time. I could count vast numbers of Japanese bombers at almost any hour of the day.

As we continued our trek up the island, I noticed an abandoned freighter burning off shore. The freighter was obviously an earlier target of the large formation of bombers who were unloading their tons of bombs over Corregidor Island, located a few miles away in Manila Bay. As the planes circled back and forth seeking new targets, occasionally some of them would drop a few spare bombs on the burning ship. The thought crossed my mind that they must get some sort of thrill from explosions. After the Japanese attacks on our airfields, I had grown weary from them, to say the least.

We bivouacked at Cabcaben for about a week; then we moved north again. About midway up the peninsula, our leaders halted our advance and directed the 31st Squadron and other air corps units, along with the 31st Infantry and the Philippine Army, to set up a defense line. That defense line, which was in the shape of a horseshoe, reached all the way across the peninsula, from Manila Bay to the South China Sea. An effective group of field artillery units supported us from behind, so with the Japanese on three sides and sharks and the China Sea on the other, we dug in. We could not go anywhere, but we could resist and make problems for the Japanese forces who were obsessed with the Philippine Islands.

The assignment for the 17th Bomb Group was to guard and prevent Japanese troops from crossing a mountain trail and to flank the American defenses from the rear on the west side of the peninsula. It soon became obvious that we could concentrate our defensive forces by pulling back south about five miles for a shorter perimeter since the mountains were impassable on the west part of the peninsula. We could link our defense from the steep mountain slopes on the west to the eastern bay coastline. These natural barriers allowed us to utilize a smaller number of troops.

The forward position of our lines was maintained with flooded rice paddies and barbed wire fences. This strategy had the general appearance of a well-engineered trap set up to engulf the Japanese forces when they entered the narrow perimeter. Once they were within eyesight, then our artillery would take them out. Without planes, modern weaponry, and supplies, we not only utilized but also depended upon the rugged terrain to assist us in our defense of Luzon Island. The terrain was tough going, but it saved our lives many times over.

After the Japanese Navy sank our Pacific Fleet at Pearl Harbor, the ships' convoy of airplanes never arrived to be uncrated. We were in possession of two old P-40 fighter planes, and we felt ourselves fortunate to have located the boxes of World War I old Springfield bolt-action rifles that had been stored and pickled in Cosmoline for the past twenty years. We had learned how antiquated and out-of-date the bolt-action rifles were during our firearm training after the disastrous attacks by the Japanese, but they were all we had. In contrast, the Imperial enemy had men, planes, and mechanized equipment; and they were in control of the large stockpile of food supplies they captured in Manila.

Time and again we looked for food supplies and reinforcements to arrive. They said, as the rumors went around, "There are hundreds of ships with thousands of planes waiting off the coast ready to come in." Then Tokyo Rose began a routine daily broadcast to our radio units with the song, "Waiting for Ships That Never Came In." Suddenly, we realized the entangled circumstances we faced—*cut off!*—without equipment and supplies and near starvation. Eventually, we became known as the "Battling Bastards of Bataan."

Hunger

Like a terrifying nightmare, the duration wore on. The US Quartermaster food supply to our unit was almost nil. For my squadron of 110 men and officers, we received three pounds of rice, three cans of salmon, and three loaves of bread. After mixing all the ingredients and cooking into a rice, bread, and salmon pudding, each man received his share of two tablespoons for each of the two meals that we received daily. There was a nervous situation for everyone at the front—Hunger!—the nagging, physical, and mental, pain of something lacking that was ever-present, even when mortar shells and dive bombers were molesting.

"Plenty of food to keep a cat alive; we'd better do something, or we'll starve to death," my pal Dan said. He and some of us often stayed together while hoping to hear some good rumors that were newly in circulation.

"There must be some food somewhere," Bob said as he stood and then desperately exclaimed, "We've got to go searching by moonlight and in the twilight! What's the difference, dying one way or the other?"

That was the desperation that sent us near the Japanese lines—scavengers of the fields and forests. With luck, we sometimes found edible roots, very scattered, and after long searches, small amounts of fruits. We even resorted to cooking lizards and monkeys if we could find and snare them. Soon, however, something to eat grew harder and harder to find. There was nourishment in juice from chewing the sugar cane when we could find it; then the Japs decided to burn the cane fields.

Hunger! Always! And with little rest, after spending half of our off day away from the outpost line to dig trenches, I found some time left to look in the stacks of rice straw and separate the grains of rice that had been left. With a stack of straw piled on a khaki shirt spread out on the ground, I found that the heavy GI shoes I wore were beneficial for thrashing rice. Combat readiness and watchfulness were paramount as almost constantly the enemy planes were overhead, and the artillery barrages were pounding our lines, making any relaxation almost an impossibility. Still, we foraged for food.

After a twelve-hour patrol every other night to a no-man's-land outpost, sometimes there were moments of leisure. It was then in the shade of an old mango tree that I found time for reading my small Bible while at the same time watching for dive bombers. My foxhole was only a few steps away, which gave me a bit of security. The words of the Bible offered me hope as well as a respite from my circumstances, moments my mind could forget the bitterness of combat while there was quietness and peace until the rattle of machine-gun fire started again. The reading and reflection also took my mind off the hunger.

This Bible was my only reading material, and the longer I read and delved into its depths, the more I agreed with many of the great theologians and philosophers: this certainly must be "the greatest story ever told," as the great book is often described. The reading that I had begun after we departed from

San Francisco on the *Coolidge* continued to offer solace for me during these desperate days and nights. In three months, I had finished reading all the books, from Genesis to Revelation.

At the time, the usefulness of the Bible passages seemed to have a more expressive significance, meaning that was appropriate for the circumstances in which I now found myself. The biblical history of man's creation and the old patterns of man's strife were just as common in our orthodox, so-called Christian society of modern times. In other words, they spoke to me in a way most meaningful for my condition at the time; and because of my condition at the time, I believe I listened more intently than I might have back home in America.

I thought about the folly of mankind fighting wars, with the ever endlessness of conflict. Since Cain killed Abel, the intrigue of conflict continues its offer—illusions that for centuries have plagued mankind with a falsehood of political ethics to take something that belongs to others. In dismay, we are reminded of that which is written: "And ye shall hear of wars and rumors of wars" until the end of time (Matt. 24:6, King James Version). The first part of the passage was troubling even though the passages advised not to be troubled or to worry, which was a difficult task as I pondered what the immediate future might bring. I had no idea.

On March 14, 1942, after night patrol from an outpost, I returned to my bunk in our jungle home. Here a dense thicket had afforded accommodation for my well concealed bunk made of bamboo poles and decked with rice straw; my foxhole was only about twenty feet away and handy to get to when artillery shells made barrages in the area. On this morning I was tired and hungry upon arrival back to the main defense line. Something to eat was the priority. In haste I detached my pistol belt and field gear.

Soon, I located Dan about a hundred feet out in the mango grove. His peanuts were beginning to roast, spread on a hot piece of tin that had live coals beneath it. Following his example, I also put my peanuts on to roast. With these edibles for our morning enjoyment, the day seemed much brighter. While passing through an old farmstead during the late afternoon the day before, we had located a few peanut vines that were still growing. About two pints of peanuts were gathered from there. That was a real find!

Surprise Attack

No sooner than the peanuts began to roast, there were sounds of planes. After many bombing runs, we had learned to detect the sounds that indicated they were coming in to make a dive.

Dan said, "Run! Down behind the log!" Shrilling and screaming, the bomber dove; then came the explosions!

A cloud of dust and smoke filled the air; we knew this was a close call. Concussion that made the hair on the head rise gave us all a shake. We had been *blasted*, but the bombers had missed their targets again. We were still standing. Looking back toward our lunch, I saw the peanuts fallen over on one side, and they were burning—our food, the most important concern of the day, was burning up. The bomb had missed them, but the fire was going to take our meal away from us. With this urgent need, I rushed back for the immediate recovery of the peanuts.

At that point, we realized the damage the bomb had inflicted on our jungle camp. Dust and smoke filled the air as I moved to locate the bowl craters. In the direction of my bunk, I could hardly see for the thickness of dust. Coming to an opening that was cleared of bushes and small trees, I did not recognize the place at first. However, as the dust began to settle and I looked about, I could see an opening, about a thousand square feet in size; and the opening was in the exact spot where my bunk had once rested in a dense thicket. There, in astonishment, without words to say, I stood still and stared. Nothing remained to see but a hole and the clearing in the jungle.

After walking over near the middle of the area, I stopped and stood motionless. Then the thoughts began to streak through my mind of the many times—so many times!—in the past weeks when dive bombers had made fake dive runs over these locations, when the planes had made the runs without releasing the bombs. As I stood and remembered how I had lain there on my bunk and watched them through the openings between the branches of the trees because I had become tired of running to the foxhole on the false alarms, I realized I had become neglectful. And it almost cost me—and my buddies. I recognized at that moment how dependent all of us had become on the dense undergrowth and the thick cover the trees of the jungle provided us.

I began to look here and there for some signs of my belongings. Finally, I sighted my .45-caliber automatic pistol hanging in a shredded leather holster about twelve feet high above me. My pistol belt had been caught in the branches of a nearby tree. The familiar spot was now in disarray, as was my mind. While I continued to survey the scene, the realization struck me at last: on the very spot where my bunk had once been located, there was now a bomb crater.

And then a traumatizing thought flashed through my mind—my Bible—my personal and treasured possession had lain directly in the blast of destruction. I wandered around, dumbfounded, hoping to find pages, even bits of the paper pages, among the debris. As I looked around in disappointment and despair, friends came up and joined in the search.

We hoped to find my Springfield rifle; however, after surveying the area, we observed firsthand how the instantaneous fuse of a fragmentation bomb causes almost complete destruction of everything above the surface as it spreads out from the point of impact. The crater in the ground was only about two feet deep, but around its outer fringes the small trees and vegetation had been sliced in two, about four inches from the ground. The surroundings seemed to have been swept clean, with the decapitated vegetation and the bare ground sending a dire message to all of us as we looked at the crater site and then at each other.

For a moment, we stood stupefied. Then we looked around at each other, still dazed, but with the relief in all our faces indicating, without uttering a word, that we all understood the repercussions of what might have been had the bomb landed closer to any one of us. The peanuts and the decision to roast them a short distance from our bunks and foxholes had probably saved our lives. We had dodged the proverbial bullet—a really big bullet!

A bit animated, we returned to our search. My helmet, now only shreds of steel, was soon found, a grim realization that I was now without a hat, and very likely without any of my other belongings. After a while, I told my buddies I would wander around a bit more and that they should go ahead and get back to their duties and tasks. I think they believed, like me, it was a hopeless search.

Nevertheless, I headed off on my wanderings alone, venturing at last into the deeper forest to see if just by chance anything had been blasted farther than we thought. In a short while, well before the morning was over, my perseverance paid off. I could not believe my eyes when I spotted the little green cloth bag in which I always kept my Bible. There it was, sitting upright, about 150 feet in the undergrowth of the forest.

Dare I hope, I remember thinking, that my Bible would still be in the bag? I reached into the depth of the bag, and to my great joy found my Bible still inside as if nothing had happened. In fact, there was no sign of damage, not even a scratch on the book itself. The metal tag on the zipper closure was missing, but that was it. My helmet had been shredded, my gun belt ripped to pieces, and a week later a piece of my rifle barrel was also found in the jungle. However, in some way, through a miracle of sorts, the Holy Bible survived. Amazing!

Unknown to me at the time, this would not be the only time my Bible would be lost to me and then later found through unusual circumstances. My Bible always found its way back to me, or in this case, I found my way back to it.

The realities and implications of this loss and recovery have since been incomprehensible to me and a source of much contemplation. At first, of course, my joy of recovery shrouded any serious consideration of the event. As days passed, however, I pondered the feasibility of one object confined in a very small space with my other belongings surviving the blast inflicted by the bomb. Even more remarkable was the pristine condition in which I found my Bible. The occurrence and the facts were sufficient for the complete amazement of my imagination.

As a result of our "close call," my group and I immediately put into practice a more careful alertness when the drone of the Japanese planes approached, adopting the philosophy that all planes equaled the likelihood of another close call. In addition, we were extremely careful in the selection of our next jungle thicket in which to build our bunks and dig our foxholes. We worked at finding a spot where the leaves of the trees and undergrowth concealed even a small glimmer of sky. Of course, we had presumed our original home was safe and after discussion decided it was probably the smoke of the fire from our roasting peanuts that provided a target for the Japs. I think it would be safe to say we had a consciousness-raising experience. I know I did.

With days turning into weeks, conditions worsened for us; still, we continued to fight. We were near starvation, but we still spent our days trying to hold the line and to avoid the Japanese planes. When we finished our posts, we continued to forage for food although we had just about cleared out all the fruits and the nuts. When the bananas were gone, we found a way to eat other parts of the plant. We were slowly starving to death, but we didn't know it or even think about it at the time. We foraged and we fought.

Then in March, we heard that General Douglas MacArthur, who had retreated to the fortress of Corregidor across the bay, had been ordered by President Roosevelt to abandon Corregidor and go to Australia. We didn't think he would leave us there, but he did. Not even Douglas MacArthur could argue with the president. That didn't do much for morale as MacArthur was the hope of many of the defenders of Bataan because most of us knew his history with the islands. He had been raised in Manila while his father, General Arthur MacArthur, was stationed there. Everyone knew Douglas MacArthur loved the islands and its people, and he loved Manila. The people of the Philippines also loved General MacArthur.

Not everyone admired MacArthur though. In fact, many hated him, believing him to have more flaws than heroic qualities. To some, when they heard MacArthur had vowed on his arrival in Australia, "I came through and I shall return,"[5] he was making a promise he intended to keep. To others, it was the bravado of a soldier with a huge ego who loved the fight but also loved the fame and adoration.

AMERICAN P.O.W.
#1000

SIX

Surrender and the Bataan Death March

After MacArthur's exit in March, we fought on until the first week of April. Barely surviving, we held on while all the signs indicated we would not be able to last much longer. Then our line of defense broke down, and we heard General King was going to surrender. It was right about the time when we were driven away from the line that we heard about King's surrender plans, and the line never got reestablished. We—the 27th Squadron—were driven back down to the southern area of the island near Mariveles on the upper edge of the landing strip. That was where we were on April 9, 1942, when we got the word that Major General Edward P. King had surrendered us to the Japanese, giving us the distinction of being the largest group of American soldiers ever to be taken captive. The group actually consisted of approximately 12,000 American soldiers and 66,000 Filipinos, who were allies of the United States.

Very soon after that news, we learned that the surrendering American soldiers were to assemble around or near the Mariveles Landing Strip. I don't know how many were there when we arrived, but I do know that none of us knew what was going to happen. I wasn't afraid at that time. Ray and I had thrown a load of guns down the mountain before we headed down there as we had been instructed. No one wanted the Japs to get extra weapons; they had plenty of their own. We had also heard that we should get rid of any valuables and Japanese money. We were just getting ready for we didn't know what. Nobody knew anything. After a short period of time passed, more and more soldiers began to show up, and they continued until the area was wall-to-wall American soldiers.

Oddly, as I thought about it many years later, we had never considered the concept of "prisoner of war" during our months of fighting. It wasn't until someone passed the word that we might all be taken prisoners of the Japanese that it became a possibility in our minds. We didn't know who it came from. We had been at Cabcaben, and we heard it through a messenger. Right around that time someone started a rumor that if captured, we would probably be returned to the United States if the US government would pay ten dollars per soldier to the Japanese government. That didn't even sound believable to most of us. Also demoralizing was the idea that the worth of an American soldier equaled a mere ten dollars.

I remember a conversation I had with my buddy Ray as we tried to figure out what our future held. "I must confess, Ray," I said, "there is something off about this situation. We have been told by the military command that the Japanese do not take prisoners." That was the word we got during the time we were under siege, when we were holding fast until the breakthrough, during which the western section fell.

"Guess we'll see soon, buddy," Ray responded. Like me, he was not sure what to think or to expect.

Now, with Japanese guards appearing on the Bataan Peninsula, it didn't look good to me. The Japs had driven us all the way to the tip of the Bataan Peninsula—a jump-off place into the sea. With our forces scattered throughout the lower half of the peninsula and many of them moving to the south after word of the upcoming surrender, the same question echoed in many soldiers' minds: "How can we trust them now if we did not trust them then?" But the answer to that was clear; we had no choice.

After a few hours, hundreds, then thousands, of American and Filipino soldiers had gathered on and around the Bataan Peninsula, and the Japanese guards were everywhere. Roy, my cousin, was with me most of the time. We just followed the instructions of the guards. They said to go down and line up, so we did. They began to check for guns, and they took any jewelry, money, and knives soldiers had on them.

Fortunately, the word had been passed through our soldiers to get rid of any Japanese money or products before the guards arrived for the shakedown. That turned out to be some of the most valuable advice we had received in a while. If the guards found items that might have been carried by a Japanese soldier killed by an American, it would be dangerous for the holder of those items. This proved to be tragic for one American officer who had obviously not received the word to get rid of Japanese money. We were not in the vicinity of this horrifying execution when it happened; but word spread later that as soon as the Japanese guard found the money, he went berserk, shouting and bouncing around. Before the soldier knew what was happening, another guard pushed him to his knees on the ground, and with one decisive slash the wild, frantic guard beheaded the man. It was an event that got the attention of all when it was retold.

When it came time for me to be checked, I took my billfold out and showed it to them, but it was empty. No one in the world wants an empty billfold. I had taken my money out and slipped it in slits in my shirt collar and waistband that I had cut with an old knife. It was one blade only, and it was the only questionable item I had on me. I had dug a hole in the ground earlier so they wouldn't get it. Because there were so many American soldiers, this process took a long time. I would call it confusion and loosely controlled chaos.

During the search, the one personal item the Japs failed to take while we were being searched was my Bible. The guard examined it and then returned it to me. I was relieved since I knew I would need this Bible in the days ahead. It was a small Bible; but in the weakness and hardships of the long march, even the smallness of this object became weighted and burdensome. I was hoping, however, to retain this possession until the last. It contained a passage personal to me, the words of the psalmist: "The Lord is my shepherd . . . . Yea, though I walk through the valley of the shadow of death, I will fear no evil" (Psalm 23: 1-4, KJV).

These words I kept foremost in my thoughts even though many times, in near complete exhaustion, I feared that I would have to discard this valued possession because of the extra weight it added in the small bag that hung around my neck. I remember to this day the degree of fatigue my army buddies and I suffered on that road. It was a fatigue I had never before experienced or imagined. I was accustomed to working in the hot sun in the cotton fields at home, but there I could stop and rest and get a drink of water. On the march, you just kept going, willing yourself to put one foot in front of the other and at the same time telling yourself you could do it. Thankfully, the faint—a total collapse—did not happen until several days later upon arrival inside the gate of Camp O'Donnell.

The Death March Begins

After the chaotic searches—on the next day, April 9, 1942—the Japanese guards began marching the large numbers of prisoners north along the National Highway of Bataan. Members of the 27th Bomb Group began the march from around the Mariveles Naval Air landing strip. It was a totally different march up the dusty highway than the one on Christmas Day when we first arrived on the Bataan Peninsula over three months before. At that time, we were following the orders of our American military leaders; on this day, our future lay in the hands of the Japanese. It was a horrible thought.

Then around noon, about four or five hours after the start of the march that morning, the Japanese guards stopped our group in a large open place for a roadside sit-in. Up until that point we had not been allowed to stop for anything, with the guards surrounding the lines and constantly pushing us to move forward. At last, most of us thought, we're going to get a little rest. The guards began immediately shouting out orders, telling us to sit in close formation and requiring us to remove all hats and head coverings. The sun was blistering, but we were not allowed to place a towel or anything above our heads to keep the sun from the upper part of our bodies.

The sadistic guards, who had repeatedly refused to allow us to stop for water from the nearby streams we passed, called this a "sun treatment." Thus, we sat bareheaded in the hot tropical sun, which was regularly around 110 degrees in the middle of the day on the National Highway. As surreptitiously as possible, we rubbed our heads and faces to give a little shade with our hands. The POWs who refused the sun treatment and replaced their hats were beaten on the head with a rifle, and sometimes they were bayonetted for not cooperating. This was not the first times the guards had used their rifles and bayonets.

Shortly after the start of the march, the killing, harassment, and torture began. At times, the guards clubbed men to death; at other times, the guards used their swords, bayonets, and pistols. There seemed to be no organized plan or reason. It is estimated that almost four hundred men from the 19th Philippine Army Division were beheaded, primarily with sabers. A Japanese interpreter explained, "We are doing this because many of our men have died fighting against you." He didn't appear to factor in the number of our men who had been killed by Japanese soldiers. That was the thought going through my mind, but I knew better than to speak it. I wanted to survive.

Unknown to us, we were being marched to a prison camp in the northern part of the island. Other prisoners were picked up along the way if they had not made it to the tip of Bataan before the march started. Those who had gathered at the tip of the peninsula or near Mariveles Air Field marched approximately sixty-five miles to the first prison camp, if they made it—and many did not. On this first day of the infamous Bataan Death March, those of us who survived wondered if we would make it through the next day.

On foot, we struggled back across the battlegrounds. Nothing was left of the countryside but the devastation of defeat. The destruction from the bombing all along the way was unbelievable, nothing like the beautiful, tropical countryside we had seen on our first march up the highway on Christmas Day. Even the natives who once lived there were leaving and coming along with us; they had lost everything. Without food and water, little was left in the will to resist, only a struggle to endure. One word was on everyone's tongue—"water." That was the conversation topic when a few words were spoken among us. Even a few words expended energy needed to make it to the next stop where there might be a chance for some water.

After the second day's march, I stood in a line all night for some water, waiting in that long line to find when I finally arrived for my turn that the artesian fountain offered only a small trickle of water. The monsoons and rain had not begun yet, so it was terrifically hot. After a short wait, there was the fifteen-mile hike along the hot road before we could count on any rest during the next guard change. Each time that happened, I prayed for a less angry, violent guard. And there were some who did not relish killing starved, exhausted men just for entertainment. However, some were obsessive about punishing the Americans whenever the chance arose. Sometimes, the most savage ones didn't need a reason. I decided early that I needed to become as "invisible" as possible, disappearing out of the sight of the guards when feasible.

Many of my friends didn't make it through the second day. I fought to keep the sadness and the shock of their senseless deaths out of my head. We had been in a near starvation state for the last four months. Now, asking weak, hungry soldiers to march in the tropical climate of the Philippine Islands without water was a death sentence for many good men who would never return home. At this point soldiers began falling out, passing out from a combination of heat, exhaustion, starvation, and dehydration. If they fell and didn't get up, the guards bayonetted them or shot them and left them in the ditches alongside the road. We learned not to stop and help them; those who did were whipped or beaten with clubs or, in some cases, suffered the same fate.

At other times, those of us who were able were forced to bury the dead by the roadside. Many who were not dead but near death were buried as well, with their horrible moans and cries clearly distinct as they struggled for their last breaths. It quickly became clear the guards would be swift to inflict pain in any way possible and expected strict obedience. Those soldiers who suffered from dysentery who attempted to head to the roadside to relieve themselves were ordered to return. If they did not, they were shot or bayonetted.

During the march, I spent most of the time running. Once, when I was nearing a ditch with water in it, I rushed up to scoop up some water. Then, I saw the guards coming from behind with fixed bayonets to prevent us from getting a drink, so I bolted away to escape the wrath and the bayonets of the guards. Most of us were not there long enough to quench our thirst anyway. One day I was lucky to find a bottle of iodine in the road, so from then on, I used it to purify the filthy water we were forced to drink. None of us ever figured we would drink muddy water, but we did it to save our lives. The thirst is impossible to describe when you haven't had water for hours, or only a few swallows in a day. And always the heat surrounded you.

When we at last reached San Fernando, the first sight of the train brought a sigh of relief to us as we assumed we would now be able to get off our feet, or so we thought. We foolishly believed that after we were loaded into boxcars, we would get a little rest. What actually happened was that so many POWs were crammed into each boxcar, and we were standing so close to each other, that we might as well have been a bundle of toothpicks squashed into a box. They stuffed close to a hundred men in a boxcar built to accommodate forty. Of course, the air was stifling. With so little air and so many men, I feared we would all suffocate. Many of the weakest became delirious and passed out, or they went into a coma or an unconscious state standing completely upright. Those poor souls never made it to Camp O'Donnell; they died standing up in that train boxcar thousands of miles from home.

Around midmorning, probably nine o'clock at home, the train arrived at the town of Capas. Those who were still breathing engaged in a desperate struggle to escape the smothering boxcar; then we proceeded to march again. The tropic air was so hot it seemed to be moving in front of my eyes. After the approximate eight-mile march from the town of Capas, we assembled into large groups in close formation. As I looked at the wretched, emaciated condition of those around me, I marveled at what a man can endure. Then I wondered how much longer any of us would last.

A Filipino and a Japanese officer approached, attempting to force the prisoners along as the long line of prisoners began to arrive at Camp O'Donnell. Their instructions indicated they were unconcerned about the condition of the POWs. Some men in my group were no longer able to stand, a few depending on a buddy to hold them up. Although our expectations were not high after our "March of Death," no one could have guessed the future would be worse.

"If something would just happen to let me get off my feet for a while, man, they hurt. Can't believe my legs could get any more tired," Ray said. Weary beyond belief myself, I knew what he was talking about.

Word was passed up and down the column of men to expect another check by more guards. Ray and I were two steps apart when he said, "The front of the column is entering the gate. Who's giving the orders?"

"Well, what do you know? A turncoat Filipino with the guards—just another Judas," I answered.

We heard someone behind us saying, "That's another one of the patriotic citizens from the underground. They sprang up after the Japanese victory. Look on his left pocket; see the white flag with the rising sun in its center."

Then still another voice behind us responded, "You know, he is big and important now, a snake in the grass a few days ago. Look there! Over just inside the gate, three more of them."

I was not surprised. You will always have traitors who stand ready to sell out their friends and countrymen for a few pieces of silver and favors.

"Ray," I said, "those fellows have been with us all the time, haven't they? We just didn't know they were on the other side."

We later learned that before the breakthrough on Bataan, for fifty centavo (twenty-five cents in American money), those spies were sending up flare signals along our trenches at night.

They were sneaking around our gun positions and sending up flares to signal the enemy artillery observation spotters.

"They're not all here," Ray said. "The machine gunner I was with finished off two of them reflecting their mirror signals to a Japanese plane one day."

Sure enough, as expected, when we moved closer to the gate, we saw the turncoat Filipinos wearing the Japanese flags while they walked up and down the long column of American and Filipino prisoners.

Repeatedly, they shouted, "Let us see your money! You will be searched until we find everything in your possession."

Besides my Bible and dog tags, I didn't have much left. The material of my shirt was slit with a razor so the bills could be folded the width of the collar. As I looked to the side, Japanese soldiers with rifles and a Filipino were taking two Americans to the guardhouse at the gate's entrance; each was given a shovel. Soon they left the other prisoners and went over the hill.

One of the natives who had turned traitor said for all to hear, "The two Americans—they gone to dig graves—they carry Japanese money in their pockets. They take the Japanese coins from the dead Japanese soldiers' pockets."

The Japanese guard shouted, "Killed! They must be killed! Understand! If you have Japanese money, you will give it to the Japanese soldier too."

"Thank goodness," I thought, "the dumb, two-faced, double-crossing illiterate Filipino who is a traitor to his country—now he is double crossing the Japanese, passing the information on so freely." I hoped my fellow American prisoners who had Japanese money would have the opportunity to toss it, unnoticed, into the roadside ditch before the inspectors could reach everyone.

I realized at this time that I was carrying one extra item along the chain with my dog tags—a piece of shrapnel about the size of a battered .32-caliber pistol bullet with a hole drilled through this broken-edge piece of metal ore. The earlier guards had overlooked or disregarded it, but it got the attention of the O'Donnell captors through five prisoner searches and the inspection of the individual Japanese guard, asking "Ninee Ka!" I didn't know what "Ninee Ka" meant, but it was easy to understand he was asking for an explanation of something.

"Ninee Ka"—"Ninee Ka"—the guard continued, standing there chirping, "Ninee Ka"—"Ninee Ka," sounding to me like a talking bird.

At the same time that he was "tweeting," he was turning the shrapnel around in his hands, looking over and under it. Was there something I could do? My mind raced. I hastily pointed to the ground where there were some rocks, the weight and color of which clearly indicated iron metal, but the Jap shook his head—"Worthless"—"Was it a rock or stone?"

"No!" I answered.

Then, eager and impatient, the guard asked, "Gold?"

"No!" I answered again.

I soon realized my shrapnel was getting too much attention and was now expecting the rifle butt to come down across my head any moment. Everywhere I looked there were guards either in confrontations with other American captives or inflicting beatings on them. They were just looking for excuses. At last, the guard seemed to believe me that the metal was not gold, but he took it anyway. I was glad to get it out of my possession and avoid a close call on this first day at Camp O'Donnell.

AMERICAN P.O.W.
#1000

SEVEN

POW Camps

Camp O'Donnell

C amp O'Donnell was a death camp, as they had made the plans for it to be that kind of place. This was evident shortly after arrival. At first sight, in a heat so merciless the air continued to move in front of me, the grass-covered huts that sprawled over low rolling hills appealed to my imagination: my mind conjured up shady places to sit; was there clean water somewhere in this region? My imagination deluded me. In actuality, our new home was a half-completed Filipino Army camp with shacks and a few guard towers around the edges. No shade or rest—this was only a new chapter for the American POWs, with disease, starvation, thirst, and death silently waiting for us around every corner, day and night.

After our arrival at this vile place, General Momma, who was the head of the camp, held all the captives standing in the hot tropical sun for half the first day. The date was April 14, 1942. After we had finished the last leg of the heinous Death March, we were then required to stand in close formation without drinking water until midafternoon of that same day. After this length of time, we all began to weaken, and anxiety began to replace the small bit of optimism we felt at surviving the march. We had made the destination, but we had been standing without water for hours.

It appeared that some delay was preventing introductions. What was happening was that a few of our men were no longer able to stand; their legs just folded as they went down. I realized my legs too were weakening, and I began to wilt; but I forced myself to straighten up. The fallen were soon visited by a Jap guard who delivered a few strokes with his rifle butt or a face stomping with the hobnail shoes they all wore. This would stimulate anyone to stand if his feet and legs had enough strength to stand; those who could not stand were carried away. I did experience a faint, but it was after we were finally released to find the place we would sleep. Finally, a Japanese captain and a Filipino interpreter appeared.

The Japanese captain stood and lectured to us for hours while the Filipino delivered the interpretation—a repetitious message, with roaring insults, as he boasted of his nation's conquest of the sick and hungry Americans. He told us the Orient was for Orientals and that Americans had invaded their territory. He told us the Imperial Japanese Army would drive the invaders away. I never forgot one pledge the Japanese captain made during his speech at the "reception" on our arrival at Camp O'Donnell, especially the finality of five words.

He said: "You will all die here." At the moment of his speaking, the words were ominous, but they were words of the enemy that I had come to know on the march; and I took hope in the fact that I had survived thus far. After only a few weeks, however, I began to believe that he was right. Even after two and a half years of the POW experience behind me, the words still echoed in my head, in my sleep, and in my subconscious. Even many years later, an incident or a situation related to my past would bring the chilling statement back into my mind, and I would envision the venomous look on that merciless, war-hardened face. At those times, I took great pleasure in knowing that his ruthless goal had not been met. Many—too many—had died, but we did not *all* die there.

The physical facilities of Camp O'Donnell were as repulsive as the treatment we received within its walls. Best classified as shacks with grass covered roofs, many of the bamboo and frame construction buildings were leaning, the wind having blown them to a partially collapsed position, with one side fallen to the ground. We had no alternative as occupants but to find a more suitable spot for rest—sleep on the ground and cover with rice straw—this as the beginning of the monsoon season came upon us. Thus, my first impression on that first day, which centered around a profound wish for a haven to provide rest and a relief from the heat, evaporated as reality quickly emerged.

Despite the deteriorating structures, however, inside the barbed wire fences, the Japanese Army imposed a rigid censorship protocol upon all printed matter possessed by the captives. This resulted, of course, in my little Bible being carried off to the headquarters building shortly after arrival. After the examination and the finding that it did not contain adverse material or enemy propaganda, a stamp of approval for good reading material was given in red ink by the Japanese examiners. This was the second time my Lord allowed my Bible to come back to me. Unknown to me at the time, this would not be the last time.

Once we were settled inside the prison gates, from that point on, the conditions were starvation and deprivation. Death was often with us on the march, but in Camp O'Donnell and Camp Cabanatuan, it was a constant. Camp O'Donnell was inhabited by ghostly, thin, and staggering humans who were dehydrated and starving. Many of our men who would have been classified as in the heavyweight class (once within the 190 to 200 pounds weight range) were reduced to only about 120 to 130 pounds after the siege of Bataan and the Death March. Likewise, those of us who had been in lower weight ranges were reduced to a much lighter range. At a height of five feet nine inches, my weight was ninety-eight pounds by the kitchen scales.

Shortly after arrival, the tropical diseases set in; malaria, pellagra, beriberi, dengue fever, and other fevers became epidemic. Dead bodies could be seen lying inside and outside the grass-covered buildings, death from both starvation and diseases. Hundreds of bodies, both American and Filipino, were regularly carried off by the burial detail. I worked on the burial detail during part of that time—a sad and disturbing job for those of us who were strong enough to carry out the job. We normally buried eight bodies in three-foot shallow graves. Some days there simply were not enough able-bodied men to bury the dead. Thus, the dead bodies stacked up outside the barracks as the stench of death penetrated the air of the camp.

In the minds of all of us was the idea that we might be in the next bunch, a chilling thought we carried with us every day and every night! It eventually became a difficult situation to find someone with enough physical strength and ability for the grave-digging jobs to get the dead soldiers buried properly. After a while, mass graves were dug that would hold eight to twelve bodies, and a mass funeral was performed after the bodies were placed in the graves and before the covering with earth.

Some of the sick and dying could have been treated and survived if they had been given medicines before they deteriorated past the point of no return, but little or no medicines were administered. Quinine, which occasionally was available, was the exception. Like others, I suspected there were medicines hoarded up by the prison leaders and guards who chose not to dispense them so they could watch more prisoners die or use them themselves. We were less than human in their minds because we had surrendered. Actually, we were surrendered by our generals, which meant nothing to the Japanese. Their Bushido creed drilled into every Japanese soldier mandated suicide instead of surrendering to the enemy.

One of the major problems was that there was not enough water to drink, not even half enough I guessed; and the water that was available was often toxic. After a few days, we were instructed to use creek water for cooking purposes and to drink. The water from the stream had been contaminated with dead bodies or the waste from those men sick of dysentery. Those unable to walk about and do for themselves stayed put in one place until death claimed them, many dying right where they had been lying on the ground for days.

I watched as some of my friends sat and leaned back against the walls of the bamboo shacks. Starved, they were unable to walk, and many were too weak to stand. Their eyes looked as if they were set with glass marbles; they did not react to the sound of my voice when I talked to them. Until death, they became recluses, even in the midst of their friends and fellow soldiers. They just sat or lay there, soaked in their own waste, as still as stones, gazing and staring into the distance, with the wall on the other side.

However, for those of us able to hang on and get about, there was a small improvement; we began receiving a couple of meals of rice per day, an upgrade but not one that greatly improved our health conditions. Starvation and disease remained with us, and it was obvious the number of captives was dwindling. Large numbers of deaths were recorded every day after we had been in the camp for only one week. An estimated number of fifteen hundred American and twenty-two thousand Filipino POWs died in Camp O'Donnell, some from disease and starvation and others from the brutality inflicted on them by the cruel, sadistic Japanese guards.

Hundreds of soldiers had died and were dying weekly, but these facts were unknown to our families, America, and the rest of the world. They were not aware that the Fall of Bataan had deteriorated into an even more desperate situation after the surrender on April 9. In an article in a weekly edition of *Life*, dated April 20, 1942, the author praised the defenders of Bataan:

> At last Bataan fell. Its defenders had won for Americans four precious months in which to strengthen the worldwide fronts. White and brown, they had done the job like Americans. But they had also done the job at a physical price that should also be appreciated by every American. . . . Far from serums and X-ray apparatus and spotless operating rooms they suffered and died in Bataan's two Army hospitals.[6]

Ironically, in the article, which was published only eleven days after the start of the Death March, the author, with absolutely no knowledge that thousands had already died, discussed primarily the pain and the treatment of the wounded soldiers who were suffering in the hospitals that had been earlier set up on Bataan. The photographs in the article had obviously been taken days before the fall. And it would be many months before the United States and the world learned of the atrocities committed by the Japanese.

Camp Cabanatuan

On July 4, 1942, almost three months after our arrival at Camp O'Donnell, those of us able to sit up and withstand a truck ride were transported to another location about forty miles away—Camp Cabanatuan—located on the central plains of Luzon Island. About a two-hour ride, Cabanatuan proved to be somewhat of an improvement over O'Donnell and its revolting conditions. Although there were more of the same types of bamboo and grass covered buildings, they were not falling and breaking down. The rice diet at our new camp, however, continued to be inadequate for about a year.

As prisoners under Oriental captors, only the bare necessities of life had ever been afforded captives and slaves. For centuries, in fact, the value of persons in the masses (i.e., the value of their human bodies) has been considered by the Imperialist leaders only in relation to the labor and work they could perform for their masters. It is not a surprise, therefore, that as prisoners, we received only the barest amount of clothing and daily food in equal amounts to each prisoner. The purpose seemed to be to starve those of us who managed to survive the diseases rampant in the camp. If they were unsuccessful in starvation of the already sickly, bony POWs, they utilized their other main weapon, brutality.

The Foursome Outside Barracks #17E

Alongside the old bamboo and nipa palm-covered buildings, an eight-foot rough mahogany plank was nailed and fastened to the woven bamboo siding about three feet above the ground. This board represented, or served as, the table from which mess-kits of rice were placed. Outward, in front of this shelf attached to the full length of the building, was a bench about two feet high and about a sitting distance from the shelf. There, on these benches, those of us who were able to walk and sit outside assembled during mealtime, and always in the same location.

This dining area, as it might be called, was just outside the bamboo-woven window, which was located opposite our sleeping location on the inside of the building. The conference and discussion of activities for the day were carried on beside the old Filipino nipa-covered barracks building. This was the place we began our days of labor—slave labor—for the two and a half years I was in Cabantuan.

After our meal, I often spent time sitting with my back to the building, with the narrow shelf as a backrest. As a manner of speaking, this was the usual daily conference position, the time when we listened to the other members tell and re-tell rumors and battle stories from back on Bataan. Most frequently, the talk was of something to eat. The banquet style meals were not the usual "stuff" for a discussion, and the tellers would invoke heavy rebuke from all listening parties. It was the sound and solid menus that attracted the attention of the listeners—good old home-cooked, family-style meals. Everyone had a favorite.

The food I never liked back home now sounded good to me. Hunger does that to a person. We talked about the waste of food back home that is common in the every-day American way of life. The thoughts were endless. Some of our fellow prisoners were controlled by these thoughts, and many died with these thoughts as they wasted away from starvation to skin and bones, and finally, death.

Our group came mostly from Barracks #17E. Besides myself, there was Jack Harrell, who was an orderly room clerk from the Headquarters Squadron of the 27th Group. A young fellow from a Polish family, he let everyone know he was from Hattiesburg, Mississippi. Jack was a loud talker who could always be heard above the others when he was in the crowd. Other members of our quan-bucket party were a white-haired gentleman we knew only as Skipper Harris and an American Indian calvary soldier known as Chief from one of the other barracks.

Chief, unlike the others of us, did not show and display the need for food, and we noticed it did not take much for him to eat and be filled. This puzzled us because the muscles of his arms and shoulders were so large that they appeared to be swollen; but they were "for real"! He did not own a shirt or jacket to wear, so when he came around, everyone kept their eyes locked on his muscles—he looked like a world champion prize fighter.

One day Jack said, "Chief, it just doesn't take much for you to eat. Tell me. What it is you got? Is it just the Indian in you?" That was exactly what he asked Chief.

Chief didn't answer so I replied, "I guess an Indian can eat a little and get by, Jack."

Since it was getting close to noon, I brought out the black smoked quan-bucket, which prompted Jack to take charge of the day's meal. "Does anyone have anything to add to the quan-bucket—I mean me and Pardue's pig weed? Speak up or be quiet." This was Jack's abrupt manner; he often sounded rude and, perhaps, didn't know it, we decided.

Skipper Harris immediately replied, "I'm going to the wood shed to heat some water for 'me-own' tea. I shall be glad to drop your quan-bucket on the fire while I am there."

"Chief," Jack said, "when are you going to find something to throw into the pot? We're not talking next time—we are in need of it today—something to stink up this pig weed. I found just enough to feed the four of us if there was salt or something to make it tasty. Do you know a cook in the kitchen you could talk out of a pinch of salt? They know you are the best hard-working wood chopper the camp has got. Just remind them of that detail."

Chief hardly ever spoke a word. Finally, he said, "I tomorrow," which seemed to satisfy Jack.

As Captain Harris picked up the black gallon bucket of raw pig weed, he said, "No water in this. I'll add some water. You Yanks still don't know how to boil or cook."

Instantly insulted, Jack came back quickly, "That may not be okay with his Majesty—his Majesty's ship captain and royal captain to the king of England—but to tell you more, Skipper Harris, I am no Yankee. I am a full-blooded Mississippi Rebel. I mean from way down south of the Mason-Dixon Line. Skipper, did you ever hear of the Mason-Dixon Line and the Civil War? And you can get it straight that I am a full-fledged Rebel from Mississippi anywhere I go."

"Yes," Skipper calmly said, "I know there used to be Rebels, but you lost the war and you are all Yankees now."

"Skipper, who told you all that? Did the king of England tell you all that bunch of baloney?"

"Yankees still say a bunch of baloney," the Skipper said hastily in an effort to set Jack straight.

Jack was not to be hushed, though, and asked, "Skipper, let me ask you—did you ever hear of places like New Orleans, Mobile, and Biloxi?"

"Yes," Skipper responded, "I sailed to those ports, I expect, when you were still a baby."

"Well, we say that is still God's Country," replied Jack, missing the Skipper's insult completely.

"And I say you are still Yankees. If you are not Yankees, what are you?" Skipper Harris said politely as he turned to leave with the quan-bucket. And with that the discussion on Yankees was ended.

After the somewhat heated discussion, the Chief and I just looked at each other and smiled. I was glad to see the Chief could smile. I had never seen him smile before. A giant in strength, he moved slowly, I had noticed. He seemed to have no fears, no worries, no dislikes, and most amazingly, no hunger. He had the cunning aspects of a gentleman and an emotionless creature. I liked and respected him.

I also liked and respected Skipper Harris. I also appreciated him as he had assumed the daily task of carrying the quan-bucket to the wood shed and kitchen where he put our quan-bucket on red hot coals and boiled his water for tea. I had noticed that the pair of khaki pants he wore were tattered and torn, with the legs cut off above the knees. He did not have a shirt to wear, but I decided it takes more than clothes to make a man—especially when the man is the captain of a ship for H.M.S. Admiralty Service. Skipper Harris, with his white, shiny hair—premature gray, I think—was a gentleman in classic manner with all the dignities of an English sea captain. His speech was a tower of refinement, and his manner smoothly glowed as a fitting symbol of England's great place in history.

Such was a typical conversation for the foursome that "dined" outside Barracks #17E where we could escape for a while the brutalities that might occur at any moment in the main part of the camp yard. As different as we were, we developed a rapport that got us through the days. Only in Cabanatuan, I decided, would a Louisiana country boy, a proper English ship captain, an Indian chief, and a hot-blooded Mississippi boy meet and share a bucket of pig weeds.

Work Details

I worked for a time carrying heavy bags of rice until dark. It was during this time that I came down with a high temperature. I was forced to continue the rice detail until it was determined that I had cerebral malaria. I did not know anything for two days and two nights, so my friends tell it. I fought it off and survived though. Knowing my family as I did, I attributed this to the daily prayers I knew they would be offering up for me. I also kept my faith in God to see me through this stormy period of my life.

During the first months of 1944, I was put to work building the landing strip that had long been under construction for the airport located in the near vicinity of our camp. They planned to use the landing strip for their "O" fighter planes if, or when, the Americans landed. The only tools and equipment we were given were a shovel, a pick, and a wheelbarrow, which I suppose the guards thought were good enough for slave labor.

I also worked on the one-hundred-acre prison farm, which the Japanese had expanded to feed the Americans. This was great news for me. Since work on a farm was a central part of my upbringing back in Louisiana, I counted this as a blessing. My primary task was to pick the fast-growing trillium weeds and gourds for the cooks in the kitchen. Prisoners who worked on the farm or the new airport landing strip were rewarded with an extra cup of rice per day.

One group of POWs taken out of O'Donnell was sent to a clean-up job on the islands, to pick up the scrap iron for recycle and reuse in the manufacture and production of war materials. Others were sent to construct and to help improve the enemy airfield installations. In one of the airfield installations, the American medical doctor from my squadron was in a forced-labor group that was digging revetements for airplanes as protective areas for zero fighter planes. While digging in the pits, the guards and the soldiers rolled five-gallon containers of high-test airplane gasoline down the embankment. Because the container caps were removed from the cans, the containers spilled trails of gasoline into the pits. The enemy guards tossed a lighted match into the trail of spilled gasoline so they could watch the doctor and the others scramble while they were burned alive in the pit.

Escapes and Punishment

As shocking as that incident was, atrocious treatment was not unexpected in any of the camps since the Japanese gave no thought to adhering to the principles of the Geneva Convention. In the camps, therefore, there was always a changing, revolving set of circumstances. Some days I witnessed friends beaten to death with their hands tied behind their backs while they were tied together with others, behind and around a fence post. At other times I watched as prisoners were led just outside the camp, forced to dig their own waist-deep graves, and then stand inside them for the execution squad. The horrors were so malicious and sickening that even though they were a constant of our daily existence, they continued to shock and horrify.

Escapes from the camp were sometimes attempted but rarely successful. It was daring and dangerous, and to those of us who had witnessed the fate of the POWs who attempted escape and then were caught, it was unbelievable they even tried. Any thoughts of escape we might have had were quickly abandoned after we were forced to view the punishment and eventual death. Usually, the escapees were quickly tracked, followed, and apprehended. They never got far. The punishment for attempting escape was always death, but the death was never quick and was always as abominable as one could imagine.

The guards also planned for the punishment (execution) to take place in as public a section of the camp as possible. They wanted to deter any other attempts, but they also wanted to continue to horrify and sicken those who had to observe it. In one particular case, the escapees were hung on posts and beaten until hardly any skin was left on their bodies, and then they left them in the sun to die. A rain came on the first night and washed away the dried blood, so the guards beat them again until blood ran off the men. They no longer had faces. The men survived for a couple of days although we wished for their death and release from the pain. Finally, they pulled them down, took them out of the camp, and shot them a short distance away so the other prisoners could hear the shots. It appeared to some of us that the guards found some perverse pleasure in inflicting as much pain and humiliation as possible whenever the opportunity arose.

One of my friends, "W," from the city where I settled down after the war was one of the few POWs that I knew who managed to dodge death after his attempt at escape. He told how he and a few others were able to slip off from the march and hide out with a band of guerillas. After one of the guerillas was captured, he took off with some of the others and hid a distance from the camp. Wakened by Japanese voices, my friend said, "I grabbed my gun and took off running, but I didn't get far. I was knocked unconscious and woke up looking down the barrel of a Japanese rifle."[7]

My buddy was certain they were going to shoot all of them, but surprisingly they gave the prisoners a choice: they could be shot there or hike fifteen miles to a truck that would take them to a prison camp. He, of course, opted for the ride. The Japanese took him to the town of San Fernando for two days of brutal torture and interrogation. If he did not give them the answer they wanted, he was hit with a black jack; then when they tired of that, they hit him in the face with a boxing glove. He told how he thought his beatings were bad until he saw a Mexican boy the Japs thought was a Filipino. They had beaten his arms and hands so badly they were swollen three times larger than their normal size. They eventually shot the boy. When they finally finished with my friend, he was sent to build an airstrip for the enemy at Nichols Field, which was considered one of the worst details on the island.

While I was in Cabanatuan, I was selected to walk guard inside the compound area as one of my jobs. For some unknown reason, a sadistic Japanese guard decided to chase me up and down along the fence attempting to stab me with his bayonet. That was the kind of cruel, harassing behavior that so many of the guards enjoyed inflicting on the POWs. I never decided if he wanted to kill another American, even though I was doing my assigned duty, of if he just found it entertaining to watch me run back and forth along the fence, panting and gasping for air. Even at night, the tropical heat was extreme, especially when you are malnourished, exhausted, and suffering from a variety of tropical diseases. He eventually gave up his little game and left me alone. Suffering from beriberi at the time, I woke up the next morning and could not move either of my legs. I couldn't even walk with a cane, which, thankfully, ended my guard duty.

A Successful Escape at Last

It was during the time I was in Cabanatuan that (unknown to any of us while we were imprisoned) a group of POWs, who had been sent from Cabanatuan to the island of Mindanao, was able to escape the Davao Penal Colony where they were held. This group, which came to be known as the Davao Dozen, succeeded in evading their captors, and they eventually made it to Australia where they informed General MacArthur of the atrocities suffered by the American POWs on the Death March and in Camp Cabanatuan. MacArthur was not surprised. As unbelievable as the accounts were, he assured the men that he knew the Japs and, therefore, knew that they were capable of the atrocities described. This was significant because it was the first time anyone had verifiable knowledge of the barbaric treatment by the Japanese.

MacArthur, who wanted to make this information public, sent three of the men, Dyess, Mellnik, and McCoy, to Washington where they were debriefed by government officials. In Washington, however, MacArthur met resistance from both President Roosevelt and others in the power structure who did not want the story out. The argument was that the Japanese might punish the POWs still in captivity. Through the years, I have also speculated that they could have worried about blame the military and government leaders might suffer from these tragic circumstances. As a result, the stories of what was happening were withheld, but only for a while. Eventually, in early 1944, the government permitted the release of the horrors American POWs were suffering, and there was a huge public outcry.

A few years after I was freed and returned home, I located an original copy of the *Life* magazine that finally was allowed to publish the story of two of the escapees, Lieutenant Colonel S. M. Mellnik and Commander Melvyn H. McCoy, as they each recounted to Lieutenant Welbourn Kelley what they and other American POWs suffered on the Death March and in the hands of the Japanese at Camp Cabanatuan. I still have that 1944 copy with their story. As sad and disturbing as it was for the families of the POWs, the stories the men told needed to be told.

The two men withheld nothing, each, in his own words, revealing the horrors they experienced at Camp Cabanatuan and the stories the Bataan Death March survivors told them. What they said was just as I had witnessed and endured myself.

In one section of the article, Colonel Mellnik described the prisoners in Cabanatuan as "the most woebegone objects [he had] ever seen. They were wild-eyed, gaunt, their clothes in tatters. Many had no equipment of any kind and some clutched at rusty tin cans, which they used as mess kits."[8] Other details, such as the stench of dead bodies as they lay outside barracks, the numbers increasing with every passing day, shocked the nation. Besides *Life*, *The New York Times* also published the story.

Lieutenant Colonel William E. Dyess, a member of the 27th Bombardment Group who had come over with me on the *Coolidge*, was another member of this daring escapee group. A skilled pilot known for his willingness to take on any assignment regardless of the risk, he also authored a book about his experiences on the Bataan Death March. Entitled *Bataan Death March: A Survivor's Account*, Dyess' book detailing the march had an even greater impact than Mellnik's and McCoy's accounts because it was a firsthand account of the brutality American soldiers faced on their march up the Bataan peninsula. Dyess described in detail the treatment by the Japanese guards, including the "infamous Japanese sun cure," men being bayonetted, men rolled unconscious "into the path of the Japanese army trucks which ran over them," and at times, unbelievably, others being buried alive on the march.[9] Dyess' book was also withheld from the public until 1944.

Ironically, Dyess did not live to see the publication of the story he so desperately wanted America to hear. After regaining his strength and returning to duty, he died in a crash during a test flight of a new plane one month before the government permitted the outrageous report to be released. His book, however, accomplished what he hoped would happen: the nation was shocked and outraged, and the people were also angry, many calling for immediate action and revenge. This was a critical turn of events, which none of us in the factories and the camps knew about until we were freed. Of course, also unknown to us was the increased worry and fear on the parents of the prisoners of war: at this time, they didn't know if their loved ones were dead or alive.

Somehow, and by the grace of God, I am sure, I made it through Cabanatuan and with some of my fellow surviving friends was sent off to yet another nightmare. This time my destination was not a camp in the Philippines but rather a camp in Japan where we would continue to labor for the Imperial Japanese Army. One of the guards said, "You are being sent to work so that Japanese men can be used in the army to go and fight the Americans." Like the others, I accepted the fact that this next stage of my journey was out of my hands and in the hands of my Japanese captors, or so the barbarians thought. I put it in the hands of my Lord. He had taken care of me so far. Why should I fear?

AMERICAN P.O.W.
#1000

EIGHT

Hell Ship to Japan

A fter two years in Cabanatuan, those of us who were alive and able were informed we were to be shipped to Japan (or Nippon, as the Japanese referred to their homeland). We were told there was an urgent need for laborers and workers in the factories and industries. As the length of the war had stretched on, probably longer than the enemy had anticipated, a great need existed to replace the shortage of manpower in the Japanese homeland since more and more Japanese were needed in the military. Thus, my fellow POWs and I, numbering between an estimated sixteen to seventeen thousand, would be sent to Japan as POW slaves to add to the slave force. We were also moved and relocated to prevent the retaking and liberation of the Americans.

The American POWs were sent first to Bilibid Prison in Manila, after which we were compelled to participate in a captive parade and force-marched down Dewey Boulevard of that city. The parade, designed to humiliate the American POWs, ended at the docks on Pier 7, the place of debarkation in Manila Harbor where we prepared to board the Hell Ship, the *Nissyo Maru*, which would transport us to Japan. The date was July 17, 1944.

The *Nissyo Maru*, like the other Hell Ships, was a merchant ship approximately four hundred feet in length that had been converted to a prisoner transport ship. It was one of the last Hell Ships leaving the Philippines with American prisoners that did not have a disastrous encounter with the American Navy. Because the Japanese did not mark these transports as ships carrying POWs, many of them were sunk by the American planes, killing their countrymen as well as the enemy. I learned after the war it was estimated that over twenty thousand of the over fifty thousand POWs transported in Hell Ships did not survive. As I thought about that percentage, I realized once again I was one of the lucky ones, or more likely, that God had a plan for my life and was taking care of me.

Not one of us understood clearly what was ahead of us as we stood among the other sixteen thousand-plus POWs gathered on the dock. All I knew was once again, I was lined up in the sweltering heat of the tropics, this time in Manila Bay in July.

The march on Bataan flashed before my eyes as the seemingly endless line stretched backward on the dock. Finally, we began moving forward toward the gangplank. When I got a clear view of the old, rusty ship we were boarding, I looked around at my fellow prisoners who had sailed over on the *Coolidge*, wondering if they were having some of the same thoughts that were going through my mind: the Japs are going to take us out to sea and drown us. This seemed plausible given our treatment thus far. Coming to my senses, however, I realized it would be much easier to execute Americans as they had been doing fairly regularly since the first day we were captured.

On the deck of the ship, we were forced to dispose of all our personal belongings except the clothes on our back, a canteen cup, and a day's ration of rice and fish issued to us that morning before we left the old Spanish Bilibid. In my possession also was the little bag that contained my Bible. As each person passed in a file, he was required to discard his personal possessions in a stack that rapidly grew into a heaping pile, which they eventually threw into a hold in the deck. When it came my turn, I sadly tossed the small green bag onto the pile of things. Giving the little bag one last glance, I turned away, accepting the fact that this, the third time I lost possession of my Bible, was the final parting.

In despair, I continued in the single file line as we were herded into the rear cargo hold of the Japanese ship. It was dark and hot, and at first, I could hardly see in front of me. When my eyes adjusted to the dark, I saw along the sides of the hold three levels of wooden tiers, almost like shelves, each about three feet in height and eight or nine feet deep. When the shelves were all filled, prisoners were forced to stand. They told us to get as close together as possible. As more and more prisoners took their places below deck, the space soon became jammed to capacity, even as other large numbers of prisoners remaining on deck stood ready for entry. It was so hot I felt as if I were being roasted in an oven. The heat overpowered me and everyone else. As might be expected, the overcrowded condition caused many POWs to faint from lack of air. To prevent mass suffocation, the guards began pulling those who were suffering out of another passageway.

With one passageway being used for the entrance and the other an upward flow of fainting men being dragged above deck for fresh air and recovery, the process must have looked like a revolving door of drunkards, some men staggering and others falling to the deck half-conscious or completely unconscious. At some point, I was carried out on deck with others who were suffocating and desperate to breathe fresh air back into their lungs. In spite of our conditions, not too much time was wasted on revival as many who were regaining consciousness and not completely "out" found that the Japanese guards were quick to use their rifle butts and bayonets to usher their prisoners back into the hold.

Shouts and yells of hundreds of trapped men filled the air as the situation worsened. Except for the presence of the guards with their guns and bayonets, it resembled a mob totally out of control. I think the dozens of Japanese guards wanted to start an execution of the prisoner mob but lacked the nerve, knowing the wrath they would face from their superiors. Their superiors would not have been concerned that POWs were killed, only that they might themselves be punished if they didn't deliver slaves for the factories.

It seemed to go on forever. About sundown that day, the guards realized that "the game was not going well" and that they were accomplishing very little. Two or three hundred prisoners were still on deck, and those in the hold could not be kept there. I really believed they were close to being angry enough to the point of firing upon the crowd. To see the contortions on their outraged faces was a horrible sight.

After five to six hours of failure to get sixteen to seventeen thousand prisoners in one hold, a ridiculous goal, the ship's captain finally agreed to transfer half the prisoners to a forward hold of the ship. This improved the conditions some but not a whole lot. We were still crammed together with an individual's space limited to standing or sitting in a crouch. To sleep at night, we looked like reptiles in a cage, lying on one another, one prisoner with his head on another's shoulder or stomach, with his legs across someone else.

Not a surprise to us was the lack of water and facilities, so the conditions only got worse, deteriorating into a disgusting situation. Once or twice a day, the guards would lower a "latrine," which was just a large bucket, down into the hold. Then after a while, they would pull it back up. They also built what they called a *benjo*, which was actually just a wooden outhouse extending over the side of the ship. We only had access to this when we occasionally were pulled up a few at a time to the top deck for fresh air. With many of the men suffering from dysentery and other jungle diseases, we soon found ourselves standing or crouching in the waste of hundreds of sick captives. The foul, nauseating odor we lived with was another vile, revolting experience and is really indescribable. I couldn't believe humans were subjecting other human beings to this horror.

In a similar manner, we were dropped a bucket of rice and water down to us. I estimate that during the entire trip I received a cup of water and sometimes one small meal of rice a day. This resulted, of course, into severe dehydration for all of us since the heat below ship was estimated to be between 110 and 120 degrees. There was no circulation of air, which caused many men to pass out or become delirious. Since most of us had been living in a perpetual state of dehydration during the death march and in the prison camps, I am surprised that men in our severe condition when we boarded were able to survive what turned out to be a seventeen-day voyage. And some didn't; they died from suffocation and were thrown overboard with weights attached to them—disposable cargo.

About a week into the trip, a stranger came around and inquired of the owner of a Bible he had found and brought up from the lowest compartment of the ship. He had evaded the security and gone below, scavenging through the large piles of discarded possessions that had been thrown in the hold as he searched for something to eat. Amazingly, he had found my Bible in the darkness, brought it up to our cargo hold, and began searching for the owner. I was squashed among some of the POWs who were sitting, crowded elbow to elbow, on the compartment floor when I saw someone within the group reach out and hand me the Bible. I sensed it with such a strong feeling that it was almost as if I had just taken a shot in the arm. Then I once again remembered that seeing is believing. And this was the third time my Bible was miraculously returned to me.

Thinking back to that particular moment of despair when I was forced to discard my Bible, I thought for sure that it was the last time I would ever see or read my Holy Bible. I never believed that I would somehow have it returned to me yet again. My head had told me that would never happen, not again—but, amazingly, it did—and its return came from a stranger rummaging for food below the deck of a Hell Ship. His find was another answer to one of my many prayers.

.

AMERICAN P.O.W.
#1000

NINE

POW Slaves in Japan

O n August 4, 1944, we arrived at Fukuoka Camp #3, which is located in the northern sector of the island of Kyshu. Upon entering, we were all given numerical identification numbers. I was the "Number 1000" captive to enter the gates of the camp, a number I retained throughout my slave days. Besides the American POWs, there were women, boys, and teenaged girls who had been brought in from Korea and the Asiatic Mainland. With this assortment of workers, I worked for one year and four days at the Yawata Steel Mill complex, a major manufacturer of the steel needed for Imperial Japan's ships and tanks. As such, the factory was the first target of the American B-29s in 1944.

On a daily basis we traveled from Fukuoka Camp #3 to the steel factory, a distance of nineteen miles one way, riding in open top railway freight cars. Every morning, except for the last Sunday of the month, we assembled in an alleyway between the "barracks" for the trip, which took about thirty minutes. Our clothing was very thin for winter wear and not waterproof, and it rained much of the time. During the winter months the camp buildings were almost unbearable without heat; thus, more than one-half of the men were ill on a daily basis. If we had a fever after coming in from the factory, we could remain inside the camp on the following day. There were no medicines available, even on the black markets, at any price.

I contracted pneumonia during the early part of February, 1945. At first, I suffered severe chest pains, but I did not run a fever and was forced to continue going to work at the factory. After about a week of this, I contracted the mumps in my left jaw, which caused me to be placed in quarantine at the POW camp. Then after about two additional weeks, my right jaw began to swell with the mumps. The result was that I spent over thirty days in the camp quarantine away from the cold train ride. I'm sure this was less about my condition and more about the possibility of my spreading the mumps. Either way, it was a blessing for me.

American Bombers over Japan

My fellow POWs and I had landed in the center of the action; but we did not know it, not at first, at least. About one week after the latest of the American captives made it to the steel factory and began working, the American B-29 bombers began stepping up the aerial bombardment of the Japanese factories and industries. Air raids became more and more frequent in our area, with the Americans increasing the daily assaults from two to three times a week. Sometimes there were three or more in a twenty-four-hour period.

The first air-raid that took place after I arrived in Japan happened about 4:30 p.m. during my second week of work at the steel mill. We had just walked from the factory to the train station and were ready to depart for the camp after our day's work. It knocked out the centralized railway terminal, and some bombs also fell in the ships' channel and the port area. We were waiting for the train and were met, instead, by a sizeable number of bombs—blockbusters, we called them.

As the large bombs exploded from the station to the waterfront, I stretched out flat on the dirt floor of the train repair shop, enduring as best I could the tremors of the shaking earth. It called up in my mind a Doom's Day situation. The large tin building took a harsh beating from the vibrations caused by the bombs. It was like shaking rocks up and down in a tin can. With my face against the ground, the shock waves from the exploding bombs bounced me off the ground in a rippling, bouncing motion that picked me up three to five inches off the dirt floor. My face repeatedly slammed the ground as I was bounced and tossed about the floor area. I said then and there as I bounced and floated around on the ground floor, "Lord, if you will just get me out of all this and I am still in one piece, I will do whatever you can find for me to do."

Retaliation

After that first air-raid, the enemy captors started inflicting tribulation and misery on the slaves as a retaliatory measure against the American planes. Beatings and harassment were day and night affairs at the Fukuoka Camp. There was no heat inside the buildings but there was routine harassment. Many nights everyone was required to go outside in the winter weather to march around and perform physical exercise. After being rushed outside for the performance, the forced exercises were frequently carried on until the early hours of the morning. We suffered many cold and sleepless nights.

The harassment was not restricted to the night. Often before going to the factory in the morning and after our return in the evening, the camp guards (the "beating" squads) would come around with five-foot-long wooden clubs and beat up on everyone they could find inside the buildings. They explained that the purpose of this activity was "to rid the captives of boredom." Another measure the guards employed in their rotation of different harassment practices was to cut back about one-half the amount of rice that we were to receive at meal times. This was repeated a few times each week.

At other times, the guards poured handfuls of small pea gravel into the buckets of cooked rice and stirred the small rocks into the food, which we did not find until we bit into them. The result, of course, was chipping and breakage to our teeth, a small aggravation when compared to the bayonetting and the beheading, but one we took home with us and lived with for the rest of our lives—for those of us who survived to go home. Many years later my dentist, who was a true patriot, commented on the damage those little rocks had done to my teeth.

By March of 1945, the B-29 air strikes were taking place several times a week. This caused the Japanese officials and guards to become even more violent, in every way they could think up. Heavy beatings were taking place all the time in the camp. It was a struggle to make it through on a daily basis. It was during this time I received one of the worst and most severe beatings I had ever gotten in the barracks. I'm surprised I survived an enormously heavy blow to the right side of my head.

In the factories where we worked for Japanese civilians there were no beatings, but there was always a constant, driving demand from the overlords for more hard work: we were constantly pushed to carry heavier loads of materials, large bricks and equipment on whatever job that had been given to us. The civilians were not malicious; they just wanted the absolute most from every POW. Never seeming to tire of making the lives of the prisoners as difficult as possible, our captors at Fukuoka wanted to impose brutality on us. Such were the conditions with which we lived until the fall of 1945.

AMERICAN P.O.W.
#1000

TEN

Return of MacArthur

General Douglas MacArthur, famous for his 1941 "I shall return" quote, declaring his determination to return to the Philippines, was and may always be, a controversial figure in the history of both World War I and World War II. He is also one of those figures who is loved and admired by many and, at the same time, hated and loathed by many others. Many of the soldiers who despised him were my army buddies. I may be in the minority of soldiers who defended the island of Luzon in the Philippines and subsequently suffered through the Bataan Death March and Japanese POW camps who can see both sides, without taking sides. He was a soldier through and through, ego and all. I write about his actions in the Philippines and after he left Corregidor because his life was so intertwined with the war in the Philippines and its effect on thousands of American soldiers like me.

Greatly revered by the Philippine people. MacArthur has been the subject of numerous books detailing his entire life, from his youth to his final days when he was recognized as one of the most admired military heroes in America. Although my daughter Gayle and her husband Mark gifted me with *American Caesar: Douglas MacArthur 1880-1964* shortly after its publication in 1978, what I initially learned about MacArthur came from my experience during my time in the Philippines. Most soldiers knew MacArthur's history with the islands and its people. He loved them as much as they loved him, and he spent much of his life there. Many might say he only loved his family and the military more.

MacArthur had retired and was serving the Philippines as the chief military advisor to the islands when he was called out of retirement shortly before Pearl Harbor. Like many who saw him as the most likely candidate, Roosevelt believed he would be the best choice to lead the Philippines if the Japanese attacked. Unlike President Roosevelt and his advisors, MacArthur was not in the Washington circle regarding all the politics taking place between the United States and Great Britain. It's even possible General MacArthur believed President Roosevelt in the beginning when he was told the planes and other military supplies were only a few days behind the arrival of American forces in Manila. The soldiers certainly did.

The Battling Bastards of Bataan and Dugout Doug

Then, Homma's forces pushed through to Manila, and we were forced to retreat to Bataan; MacArthur, to Corregidor. That was when some of us began to question when and if those planes really were coming. The following verse, written by war correspondent Frank Hewlett during the retreat to Bataan became the motto expressing the betrayal the troops on Bataan felt after being "dropped off" to fight without supplies and equipment and then seemingly forgotten:

> *We're the battling bastards of Bataan*
> *No momma, no poppa, no Uncle Sam*
> *No aunts, no uncles, no nephews, no nieces,*
> *No rifles, no planes, or artillery pieces,*
> *And nobody gives a damn.*[10]

Sadly, that was how a large number of soldiers and their families felt.

Still, there were some who believed the planes were on the way, myself included. It is amazing to me, now, decades later, that so many of us continued to believe for months that we would get reinforcements. We were living on snakes, monkeys, rodents and roots, yet we didn't give up hope completely that reinforcements were coming. Our country would not just abandon us over here in the jungle, would they? First, the ships and equipment were two or three days behind us; next, they would be arriving next week. The excuses piled up. But the planes never came.

Even more disheartening to many starving soldiers was the fact that MacArthur crossed the few miles from Corregidor to the Bataan Peninsula only once after he retreated there. That did not please a great many of the defenders on Luzon. Instead of General MacArthur, he became Dugout Doug. I don't know if anyone ever took credit as being the author, but whoever it was created a hit song for the troops; it could be sung to the tune of "The Battle Hymn of the Republic":

> *Dugout Doug MacArthur lies ashakin' on the Rock*
> *Safe from all the bombers and from any sudden shock*
> *Dugout Doug is eating of the best food on Bataan*
> *And his troops go starving on. . . .*
>
> *Dugout Doug, come out from hiding*
> *Dugout Doug, come out from hiding*
> *Send to Franklin the glad tidings*
> *That his troops go starving on.*[11]

What the starving, sick troops did not know was that MacArthur, also, was waiting for the planes and the equipment. At first, like his soldiers, he was optimistic due to the messages received from Washington declaring support for the soldiers of Bataan and praising them for the brave stand they were taking. Optimistic in tone, the messages never revealed that

Roosevelt and his strategists had given up completely on victory on Bataan. The positive messages were designed to bolster our hope and praise our perseverance so we would continue to "hang on."

Roosevelt and Churchill were focused on the war in Europe first and the Philippines second, but none of us in the jungles knew the politics of the situation until we made it back home. At that time, the feelings of those who blamed General MacArthur for most of our problems may have changed some. From my reading and study through the years, I learned that what was said about the general was true: he was arrogant and a showman of sorts, but he did keep his word. He did return. When the United States, at last (after victory in Europe), turned its eyes toward the Pacific and defeating the Imperial Japanese Empire, which had been MacArthur's priority all along, too many soldiers had died in the Philippines.

MacArthur, however, was determined to take back the Philippines from the Japanese. What we later learned was that he, other leaders, and the American forces employed a strategy called Island Hopping as a means for reclaiming the South Pacific Islands after they successfully invaded and defeated the Japanese forces. Troops would take an island and then use it as a base to take the next one. The Island Hopping was successful, but it came at the cost of many American lives. Among those islands were Tarawa, Saipan, Peleliu, Okinawa, Iwo Jima, and finally Leyte, which was the beginning of the end of the fall of Manila.

MacArthur's Return

General Douglas MacArthur's return did not occur until October 20, 1944, when he waded ashore on the island of Leyte, the eighth largest among the thousands of islands in the archipelago of the Philippines. In typical MacArthur style, he had arranged for his photographer to record the event, a photo for the history books and a photo as proof that he had, indeed, kept his word. When he reached the beach, someone handed him a microphone and he delivered more memorable, and now famous lines:

> People of the Philippines, I have returned! By the grace of Almighty God, our forces stand again on Philippine . . . Rally to me! Let the indomitable spirit of Bataan and Corregidor lead on. . . . Rise and strike! For your homes and hearth, strike! Let no heart be faint. Let every arm be steeled. The guidance of divine God points the way. Follow in His name to the Holy Grail of righteous victory![12]

Those words were broadcast by radio across the Philippines. Shortly after that, MacArthur and his group, which included the Philippine president, left the island as quickly as they had arrived. History had been made and recorded, and MacArthur needed to finish the job he had come to do: liberate his beloved Philippines.

On the same day that MacArthur stepped onto the island of Leyte, the US Sixth Army landed and was countered by the remainder of the Japanese fleet. What followed was the Battle of Leyte Gulf, which has been called the largest naval battle ever and which ended in the retreat of the remainder of the Japanese fleet. This battle would be the final time the Imperial Japanese Navy would conduct large-scale operations during World War II. The naval victory in the Leyte Gulf allowed MacArthur's forces to move eastward across Leyte, onto the island of Samar, and finally onto Mindoro. From Mindoro, they launched the invasion of Luzon on January 9, 1945. And this was probably one of the happiest days in General Douglas MacArthur's military career. He was almost home.

Ironically, the Allied forces landed at Lingayen Gulf, which was the site in 1941 where Homma had landed his forces to claim Manila and victory on the island of Luzon. Four years later, MacArthur planned to do the same. After only a few days, nearly 200,000 American soldiers were on Luzon; and MacArthur and his forces were moving toward Manila. Before they reached Manila, they reclaimed Clark Field, the Bataan Peninsula, and Corregidor; they then advanced toward the city.

The fighting was brutally difficult with deaths on both sides, in addition to a large number of Philippine citizens. The accounts I read when I returned home were as bloody and horrific as some of what we saw on Bataan. And the treatment of the Philippine citizens, especially the children, during the Battle for Manila was unimaginably cruel and inhumane. An estimated 100,000 citizens died during the battle for Manila. This proved to me that the Japanese soldiers in World War II had to be *among*, if not *the*, most barbaric and evil soldiers in the history of the world.

On March 3, 1945, however, Manila was finally liberated from the Japanese. In April, the US Army invaded Mindanao, where Japanese resistance continued until the emperor finally surrendered. MacArthur had liberated his beloved Philippines and in June officially declared his Luzon offensive ended. <u>At this time, in June of 1945, only around one-third of the soldiers MacArthur left on Bataan in 1942 had survived.</u>

None of the events that began with MacArthur's return and ended with the liberation of Manila were known to the POW slaves of the Japanese at various steel mills or factories. In October of 1944, I was in Fukuoka #3 and working at the Yawata Steel Mill and like most other POWs knew only that MacArthur had left Corregidor shortly before Bataan fell. We all hoped he and/or the chief military leaders would devise a plan to return and liberate the islands, but we were focused on daily survival and did not engage in too much speculation among ourselves. After the bombs and the surrender, we were thankful—*joyous*, in fact—to know our personal liberation would soon take place.

AMERICAN P.O.W.
#1000

ELEVEN

Hiroshima and Nagasaki

U nknown to the POWs working as slaves in Japan, the United States had developed the weapon—the atomic bomb—that would inflict so much death and devastation that Japan would be forced to surrender immediately. At least, that was the projection of the military. On August 6, 1945, therefore, the United States dropped the first atomic bomb on Hiroshima. The destruction was instant and deadly. Never had such a bomb caused so much death and desolation, but the Japanese Emperor Hirohito refused to surrender.

Because Hiroshima was farther away from the Yawata Steel factory than Nagasaki, we did not immediately hear the rumors of the first great bomb before it was dropped. However, on the same day as the bomb was dropped on Hiroshima—August 6—a warning came from aerial leaflets dropped by American B-29 Bombers as they flew over our area of the island. The leaflets gave notice that the Yawata steel factory would be bombed on August 9, and the warning did not go unnoticed by the guards or the Japanese factory workers. I noticed a change in them.

Having self-taught myself some basic Japanese, I had developed an acquaintance with one of the Japanese civilians, a shop worker in the factory who was pleasant to work with. On August 8, he secretly informed me of his fear: he said, "Tomorrow everyone here is going to die." Then he grinned and the grin froze on his face. I will never forget the fear in his face when he revealed to me that there was going to be a "big" bomb and we were all going to die. He repeated it again and again with that huge, frozen grin on his face: "we are all going to die." And that is how I have remembered him through the years. He was frightened and traumatized beyond my understanding.

Because I had no knowledge of the details of the first bomb or of the leaflets warning of the Hiroshima bomb dropped by the American planes, I did not at first believe him. I did decide to share with the others what the Japanese worker had told me. Because of the extreme terror exhibited by the Japanese, however, we—the POWs—also became infected with a fear that maybe the leaflets were foretelling our future as well.

On the morning of August 9, 1945, therefore, fear occupied the faces of not only the Japanese guards but also the POWs. Still, we reported to the factory as we did every day, but after arrival we were not ordered to work. We just waited around—waiting for something to happen. After the Japanese guards left to go to the safest places in the factory, the places where they usually went during the American bombings, we decided we needed to get ready ourselves. It was at that point we decided to dig a pit to get below the ground as much as possible to get some protection.

The warning came to pass. Around twelve o'clock noon, the heavy bombardment started; and it continued, non-stop, until about three o'clock that afternoon. The American planes dropped every type of bomb imaginable. Some of them made the surroundings shake like that of an earthquake, and countless cluster firebombs were dropped throughout the region. All the nearby towns and factories were saturated with firebombs, and daylight turned into the darkness of night as villages went up in flames and heavy black smoke saturated the region. Unseen because of the smoke, buildings were leveled to the ground, and the countryside was devastated. A close friend of mine whose number was POW #997 died as the result of a direct hit on his head from a small bomb about the size of a pint-sized jar exploding from a large canister bomb.

It was, without a doubt, the heaviest aerial bombardment I had witnessed during my time at the steel mill; the attacks were constant and endless. An estimated ten thousand people died that day, including some of my POW buddies and the Korean women slaves who had no place to hide. At the end of the bombardment, none of us knew the United States had dropped another atomic bomb on Nagasaki, a city that actually was not too distant from where we were. We were just thankful to have survived the aerial assault. We also guessed that Japan's number one steel mill was no longer operational. It, and everyone near or within, had been a major target.

After the bombing finally stopped, the officials shouted, "All Clear!" and the American POWs were told to hike to the train station about a mile away for the electric train ride to camp, about a twenty-mile journey. We couldn't wait to get out of the smoke and out of the area. When we arrived at the station, someone said, "No electricity, so you'll have to wait about an hour or longer for a steam engine train." At that moment, I realized that I had left the factory without my canteen water bottle, a necessity, at the plant and in the camp.

Immediately, without a word, I turned around and started running back to the steel factory. There were no lights anywhere to see the way back to the factory building, and the enormous clouds of black smoke consumed the space. Although I could make out the large buildings from an outline on the sky line in the direction I needed to travel, the roadway was not visible. The atmosphere was darker than night. That is the time about which I described in a separate essay as the lowest point of my POW experience, the sickening horror of stumbling over the bodies of all the dead slave women. Many of them had worked alongside us. They had no place to hide; they did not have a chance.

I made my way back through the smoke to the train station for the ride back to the camp. Many of the Japanese guards were gone. Soon, we received word the Japanese had agreed to surrender. The war was over; we had survived. As soon as the guards were gone, we moved out of the stifling heat of the buildings and slept on the ground. The atmosphere was overheated, but everyone was excited—excited but still nervous and anxious. One of the chaplains climbed up and invaded a guard tower. We laughed and decided that must have been something he had been wanting to do for a long time.

My POW friends and I were delighted the American bombers dropped the "A" bombs on Japan to stop the war. That may shock some who read that statement. At that time, however, we had no knowledge of the massive power of such a bomb or the extent of the devastation in terms of lives to civilians. We only knew what we had suffered since the fall of Bataan. What we also did not know at the time was that because of the close proximity of our camp to Nagasaki, we were exposed to substantial radiation from the bomb also. My soldier buddies and I spent around thirty-three days in the atomic bomb "fallout" zone.

There was a time I thought that an appropriate title for my book would be *Saved by the Bomb* because when the second bomb was dropped on Nagasaki, the Emperor, at last, surrendered. The fear of a third bomb finally brought to a standstill the goal of the Imperial Japanese Empire to defeat the United States and the other Allied nations. Their dream of total control evaporated. Therefore, in a sense, we *were* saved by the bombs.

No one knows how many American as well as Japanese lives might have been lost if President Truman had decided against the use of the atomic bomb and if the US military had been forced to continue the war in the Far East.

The choice President Harry Truman made, of course, has been the topic for innumerable debates for countless years since the horrific events. There were many who agreed with his choice, but there were also large numbers who disagreed with his choice. Looking back, I now realize I would very likely have been one of those casualties if President Truman had opted to fight until the United States defeated Japan; however, it was an enormous, staggering price the people of Hiroshima and Nagasaki paid for Emperor Hirohito's obsession to rule the world.

AMERICAN P.O.W.
#1000

TWELVE

Japanese Surrender and Return Home

The first thought I had when I heard the Japanese had surrendered was "home—I'm going home." And I was not the only one! There were shouts of joy and disbelief. Normally calm, quiet friends jumped around as if they had just inherited a million dollars. It was the answer to many prayers. All we talked about was the fact—or was it only a possibility?—that the nightmare we had been living was over. We had made it. Then, almost immediately there was the thought of all our friends and buddies who had not made it. That added a miserable sadness to our rejoicing. They would not be going home. My first cousin, who had passed away from pneumonia, was one of those. I wondered if I would ever be able to get their faces out of my mind.

The next thought was logistical, actually a question as to how we would get out of the Philippines and back to our homeland. We speculated as to what the military was planning and just how they would be able to find all of the survivors: some of us still in Japan, others in the jungles of Bataan, and still others in camps all over the Philippines and other Pacific islands. They had gotten us over here and pretty much left us to fend for ourselves; would they be able to find us and get us back to the USA? Would they rescue the "Battling Bastards of Bataan" and others who had struggled for so long? These were our thoughts and our speculations as the reality of where we still were set in. Thus, we waited, worried but still optimistic. Maybe this time the leaders of the United States military would remember us and come looking for us, which they actually did.

After the surrender was announced, the US military began immediately to make plans to locate and rescue the POWs in the Philippines, Japan, and other Pacific islands where they were imprisoned. One of the first steps taken was to order the Japanese to mark the roofs of the buildings in all the POW camps with the letters "PW" since this would be, largely, an operation by air at first. These markings would facilitate the location of the POWs so that they could begin to drop food and supplies to them.

Our group at the Fukuoka Camp was much more fortunate than some of the POWs after Nagasaki and the surrender announcement: both our Japanese officers and our guards fled, terrified that they might still be in danger of another "big bomb" from the Americans. This did not occur all over though. When the atomic bomb was dropped on Hiroshima, Emperor Hirohito refused to surrender, in spite of the unspeakable horror of the devastation to the city and its population. However, after the second bomb on Nagasaki, he at last (but not the next day, a couple of days later) agreed to surrender negotiations.

Unfortunately. but not surprisingly, the rescue plans and surrender negotiations meant nothing to a large number of the Japanese forces who made the decision to continue their war against America, specifically the POWs under their watch. Instead of laying down their arms, they chose to execute the POWs they guarded. That POWs were executed at this time—after the surrender—is yet another testament to the cruelty and barbarism of soldiers with no respect for human life. We heard this continued until the actual surrender on August 15, 1945.

After having been subjected to the cruelty of the Japanese military and their philosophy of the shame of surrender, we were not surprised when we heard of these executions. In fact, for quite a while there had been a rumor that the Japanese planned to execute all the POWs when the Americans finally invaded. They had no respect for the fact that we, the POWs, had not made the decision to surrender; we *were surrendered* by our generals. This meant nothing to the Japanese soldiers. They had been indoctrinated—brainwashed—to believe a soldier never surrendered. He committed suicide, or *hari-kari*. They were guided by this principle as well as the Japanese Manifesto, which delineated their purpose as a loyal soldier in obedience to their Emperor. (See Appendix 3) The Japanese Manifesto and their worship of the Emperor, however, lead them to defeat, not victory.

On September 2, 1945, at four minutes past nine o'clock, on the deck of the USS *Missouri* in Tokyo Bay, two Japanese envoys, Foreign Minister Mamorou Shigemitsu and General Yoshijiro Umezu, signed the "Instrument of Surrender," followed by General Douglas MacArthur, representing the United States of America and its allies. The document had been prepared by the Department of War and approved by President Harry S. Truman. (See Photographs) At that moment, World War II became a topic for the history books.

Rescue at Last

Amazing how word spreads, especially on a peninsula only thirty miles long and fifteen miles wide and in parts of a country where one knows only the factory and the camp that had been home for months but little about the best way to get out. After much discussion among us, we decided to just wait. Then the word spread to us that United States planes were dropping food, clothing, and medical supplies to the groups of POWs they spotted from the air. When we saw the huge B-29 planes, which usually dropped only bombs, dropping supplies by parachute, we shouted for joy, like a bunch of school kids about to get a package of candy and gifts. The air drops also included instructions, such as "Stay where you are. We will come get you." In addition, they gave the sites on the coasts where soldiers could be picked up if they were able to walk. Now that was good news!

After the air drop a couple of friends and I decided not to wait any longer. We heard the British Military and Repatriation forces were also working the rescue, so we headed out together. If we had stayed around and had been forced to rendezvous with the British military, I believe my Bible, all evidence, and everything else would have been taken for record or destroyed and burned. Perhaps, Roosevelt's decision to, essentially, overlook his American soldiers in favor of support for the British and Europe, subconsciously affected our thinking regarding dependence on our foreign allies. We wanted to be picked up by American forces so a couple of my buddies and I decided not to wait.

Thus, on August 15, 1945, a few days after the fall of the old Imperial Monarchy of Japan, through the back gate of Fukuoka #3, *I walked free*. Free from the death camp and the wicked guards who had fled, I left behind a few sordid, wretched years of beatings and torture that had helped contribute to the death of so many of my friends as well as thousands of other American POWs. Those thousands left in the mass cemeteries and crematorium urns would never walk free from the savage, barbarous Fukuoka #3, one of the largest labor camps in Japan. My buddies and I were some of the fortunate ones.

The sights we had seen inside the camp had been horrific, but so were the sights outside its walls. Everywhere the countryside was devastated and war torn from air bombardment. It was a wasteland. Even with my accented Japanese speech and in slave labor clothing worn in the steel mill, we were not recognized as American and went unnoticed through encampments of home guard soldiers. Our destination was the southern end of Kyshu where, according to the leaflets dropped with the supplies, we would find American forces. And we did find the air base occupied by the recently landed American forces, but only after a 150-mile hitchhiking and railway journey south. The trip was much longer than the sixty-five-mile death march but a whole lot more fun.

Our next trip after being rescued was an air flight to Manila where the military had set up a Depot for Repatriation about thirty minutes out of the city. (See Appendix 5) There we went through all the steps necessary to get us identified and processed, which meant what seemed to be an endless stack of government forms to complete. There, also, we were given new uniforms and shoes as well as the opportunity to rest and recuperate. We were also given a portion of the back pay we were due. If we desired to visit with chaplains and psychologists, that was offered to us too. Most importantly, they provided as much food as we could possibly eat—and water—clear, clean water. Food and water, at last—home was on the horizon.

I left the Philippines Islands on September 25, 1945. In spite of the famed beauty of the islands, leaving for the United States of America was the day that for the last two and a half years I had prayed often would come. At times it seemed doubtful, but I had "kept the faith" and never given up hope.

The Bible, which I thought was lost to me on three different occasions, left with me on the plane. We had survived.

Back in the USA

When I arrived in California on October 20, 1945, my first stop was Letterman General Hospital in San Francisco, California (See Appendix 6). There I received a complete physical and brief assessment of the effects of my years on Bataan and in the prison camps. I don't believe any of my fellow POWs arrived home *completely* healthy although we received medical care in the various hospitals where we were sent when we left Letterman. The military sent me to the Brooke Army Medical Center at Fort Sam Houston in Texas where I was hospitalized for extensive tests and treatments for the assorted diseases I had suffered. Strangely, I had developed warts on the bottom of my left foot, but they were removed and treated. As a result of my deteriorated health, I spent longer than I expected. Eager to get released, I reminded myself that, at least—and finally—I was only five or six hours from home. That's closer than I had been in nearly four years.

After that last stop in Houston, I was released to return home for a leave. Like most of the POWs, I had suffered malaria, pellagra, beriberi as well as pneumonia and the mumps. I also came home with what the doctors called chronic bronchitis, which I was told would reoccur throughout my life, and it has. Now, decades later, I still suffer with breathing difficulties. In the first years after my return, I suffered attacks that left me struggling for every breath.

The radiation exposure caused me serious problems through the years as well. When I reached fifty, I began to suffer severe pains in my arms, legs, feet, and shoulders, along with an increase in skin cancers, especially on my face where I have had numerous procedures to remove them. Two of my doctors suggested that a contributing factor to my deteriorating health conditions was likely the latent effects caused by exposure to the atomic bomb radiation fallout at the end of the war.

In addition, in the mid-60s, a lady physician with the Veterans Administration volunteered radiation exposure information with me. She related that an associate physician with whom she worked for several years had been a member of an inspection team for the Veterans Administration, and that the findings at the Fukuoka Camp indicated the camp was located in one of the most saturated areas of ancillary atomic fallout because of its close vicinity to Nagasaki and because it was coved between the mountain sloped and the sea. I actually had not heard the word *coved* before, so I looked it up and found that it refers to a nook, a sheltered inlet or a recess in the shoreline, which quite accurately described our location in Fukuoka. It was frightening to learn that. I was blessed, though, to come home at all; I know that, so I am thankful for that gift. As is often said, "But for the grace of God," I might not be here today to tell this story.

Home

When I finally made it back to Union Parish, I got a ride from the principal of Dean School, who drove me a few miles to my home. He knew my family and that I had been on the Bataan Death March and a POW of the Japanese for years. When he pulled onto the gravel drive and I saw my house for the first time in years, I vividly remember staring for a brief several seconds. That moment in time remains as one of the happiest and peaceful scenes of my life. I was home; the old home place was still there and looked just as I had remembered during my darkest days. I thanked the kind principal for the ride and got out with my bags of belongings.

On that day, as I stood and looked around at the fields and at the barns which sat back and to the side of the house, I would not have traded that house for the most luxurious castle in the world. My sister Joye remembers that she and another one of my sisters were picking up pecans in the big tree beside our house when we drove up. Joye, who was twelve at the time, said that she was in the tree because she was the oldest, and Carrie, who was only ten, was picking up the fallen pecans on the ground.

When they looked up, they saw me enter the gate, walk up the sidewalk to the porch and go in. She doesn't remember that I said anything to them; I don't think I even saw them. My family knew, of course, that the war was over and that I had survived, but they knew nothing with certainty about the date I would be arriving home.

My mother, who must have endured many days and nights worrying, and also in prayer, was speechless when she saw me—I think it could be best described as she "went to pieces" with happiness because my sisters who were still outside the house could hear her shouting and screaming. I will remember always the pure joy in those tear-filled eyes and the strength of the arms that encircled me. In fact, I didn't think my dear mama was going to let me out of her embrace. Equally joyful was my more reserved dad who looked almost as if he did not recognize me. I don't know if my huge weight loss shocked him, or if he thought, maybe, it was too good to be true. What a nightmare they must have gone through, I thought, for they had two other sons in the armed forces to pray for too. My parents were blessed because my two brothers, one of whom was a pilot, both came home.

Later, as they caught me up on the news in Union Parish, my father told me how everyone in the parish had been sickened by the news released in 1943 revealing the horrors of the march and the POW camps. Like many other parents and family of Japanese POWs, the refusal to make public the Japanese atrocities left them angry and suspicious of communication from the government. I asked my dad if they had received any of the letters I had written from the camp, and he said they had, which surprised me a little, but which I was glad to hear. Back in the camps we had been skeptical that any piece of mail we wrote went anywhere but the trash. I told him I had received letters from him during my time in the camp and how wonderful it was, even though they was brief. The prison messages were limited to a certain number of words. (See Photographs)

During my stay at home, I was not ready or psychologically healthy enough at that time to talk about the gruesome details of my march or the POW camps, and I was not pressured to do so. My family and friends, I believe, were understanding and knew me well enough to know that if I wanted to talk about my experiences, I would initiate the conversation. As a matter of fact, it was many years later after I had begun my post-military life that I could face fully the horrors of my past and begin sharing some of my experiences. I did suffer post-traumatic stress in the early years home, but I knew the God who had brought me through the POW Hell in the Philippines and Japan would bring me through the nightmares as well. I trusted that completely.

What I did share with my family and close friends was the incredible and amazing journey of my Bible. I told them the story of how I had lost or had my Bible taken from me three times in situations where its return seemed impossible, but that each time my Bible found its way back to me. I saw their expressions of pure astonishment and told them I understood their amazement—or, perhaps, their skepticism. I explained that my buddies and I felt the same way after the first incident with the bombing of our camp site. I also shared with them the great amount of time my buddies and I had spent trying to figure out how everything, literally, had been blown to bits, everything except my Bible.

As we discussed the chances of what I ultimately considered a miracle, I revealed to them that, finally, after much contemplation and prayer, I had decided it was not fate, not a freak accident, and not just chance. It was God. This was the first time I had voiced that belief out loud, but I had known it in my heart and in my head for quite a while. It was good to be among loved ones and friends who were also strong Christians who would understand.

A New Beginning

Spending time with family and lifelong friends was wonderful, but the best thing that happened after I returned home was meeting a beautiful young woman at a party in a small town not too far from my home place. Her name was Demaris Whitard, and we connected immediately, with her sharing her life and me explaining some of my time in the military. Although I did not know much about courtship, or even women, for that matter, I began to believe after only a few dates, she was the one for me. I thought, and hoped, she felt the same way. I knew also I wanted a family like the one provided by my parents. I had learned she was close to her parents and family as well.

I was no different from many young soldiers returning home from the war in the Pacific. It had been almost six years since my enlistment, and I had done my tour of duty in Hell on earth. I wanted to settle down and begin a normal life. When I worked up the courage to propose to her, she said, "Yes." And at that moment, the march, the beatings, and the despicable

Jap guards were miles away. I could live again. So, around five months after we had met, my wife-to-be and I drove with friends and her brother to a Justice of the Peace in a nearby town and became man and wife. The date was May 1, 1946. I didn't know it at the time, but we were destined to have a long and happy life together.

As the end of my tour of duty approached and as I expected, the Army Air Corps offered me the opportunity to re-enlist, providing a three-hundred-dollar bonus and the possibility for advancement. This was a difficult decision for me, considering what I had experienced on my first tour. Three hundred dollars, however, was a lot of money in those days, so I gave it some careful thought. Although I didn't plan on making the military my career, I did need a job, so I took the Air Corps up on their offer and signed on for three more years. My first Honorable Discharge on August 6, 1946 was followed one day later by my reenlistment date on August 7, 1946. I figured that by the end of those three years I would be more settled and know what career I wanted to pursue. I was to be stationed at Barksdale, which was another plus because I had enjoyed my years there before the war. The year 1946 was not only a period of change but also a blessed time: we married on May 1, 1946; I was honorably discharged on August 6; and I reenlisted on August 7.

I had found a small place near Barksdale in Bossier City before my marriage, so it was there my new wife and I settled in. The first months brought a period of adjustment as I was still suffering lingering symptoms of the many jungle diseases, especially the asthmatic and lung problems. I frightened my wife Demaris to death some nights as I gasped and prayed for the next breath. Fortunately, the hospital was near the base, so I was able to get treatment. Unfortunately, my new wife, who had grown up in a small town, did not like life in the big city. As a result, we made numerous trips home to visit, and I realized quickly that our time in Bossier City where Barksdale was located would end at the end of my service. Time passed quickly. A little over a year later, we welcomed an addition to our young family, a daughter, Janis Ann. Life had returned to normal.

We also began looking for a place to live closer to both our parents on the other side of the state. Eventually, we found two lots near Northeast Louisiana Junior College in Monroe where I intended to enroll on the G.I. Bill. Our lots were a few miles out of the city with land and trees, so we thought it would be perfect. Monroe was just the right size for us, not as large as Shreveport or Bossier City where Barksdale was located, but it did offer a hospital and a downtown shopping area. Three years after my reenlistment, on July 13, 1949, I was once again honorably discharged from the United States Air Force and resumed life as an American patriot civilian.

On my time off, I began clearing the land and putting down the foundation for our new home. When I was officially out of the service, my dad and I began building the house. My dad was a skilled builder, so he directed the work. It was not a big house, but it was just the right size for us, and we had plenty of space. The location also placed us within a short driving distance to the homes of both our parents, which was especially important to me as we had lost my mother in 1950 from leukemia.

As we were finishing work on our new home, I enrolled at Northeast, with a major in accounting and a minor in English. At the same time, I found a job selling insurance until I completed my degree. It was a demanding schedule, but I made it; and in 1954, I graduated with a bachelor's degree. Soon after my graduation, I submitted an application for a job and was hired. We also welcomed another little daughter, Gayle Elizabeth, in April, so this was a wonderful year for our family. I couldn't imagine a better life and, prayerfully, thanked my Lord for a peaceful life in a free country.

XPOW Connections

After several years, I began to hear from some of my war buddies. We had all been busy getting our lives back on track after returning from the war, but it seemed some of us had the same idea around the same time—check on the other "Battling Bastards of Bataan" that we had spent so many days, months, and years with. Like them, I had wanted to see how life was treating my friends after returning to the states. We phoned and wrote, sharing news and information we knew and planning future communications and meetings. We also met with other POWs in our area once or twice a year for food and conversation. A national organization was soon established.

After the war ended, the surviving POWs finally learned details of the war unknown to us while we were imprisoned in the POW camps or working as slaves of the Japanese. As POWs, we were too busy fighting our own wars within the camps to think much about the war in general, not that any of that information would have ever been shared. The less we knew, the better the Japs liked it. Like numerous friends I sought to know what happened in the battles not only in the Pacific but also in the European theatre. It was almost as if we had been in another world while World War II was raging around us; I suppose, in a way, we were.

I learned much from the old magazines and newspapers as I read and researched; eventually, of course, books began to be published by historians as well as survivors of the war. I purchased some and discovered that the stories were similar in most cases, some more than others. Several decades later, two nephews of American soldiers from the 27th Bombardment Group in the Philippines took on the task of uncovering the details of their uncles' service record and of their deaths since little could be found in the records. It, surely, must have taken them years, for the book provides in-depth research of what the 27th Bombardment Group endured, offering a picture of other POWs and their nightmares in the Philippines as well.

What these two family-member "investigators" produced was the most detailed research I had seen thus far on the group they labeled (in the title of their work) as "ill-fated," an apt description of an operation ironically given the code name "PLUM." The work also details, very likely, the most accurate—and shocking—numbers of those lost on Bataan. Martin and Stephenson report:

The personnel records of April 3, 1942, indicate that there were between 78,000 and 79,000 Filipino and American troops on Bataan. About 2,000 of these men eventually escaped to Corregidor. Between April 10 and June 4, there were 45,000 Filipinos and 9,300 Americans at Camp O'Donnell Prison. The difference between the April 3 numbers, minus those who escaped to Corregidor, and the Camp O'Donnell numbers indicate that more than 21,000 men had disappeared. Some escaped and others were killed during the fighting, but most died either on the Death March or from disease and starvation at O'Donnell or elsewhere.[13]

As a POW in O'Donnell who served for a time on the burial detail, I know that some soldiers were buried without their dog tags or any identification, sometimes in mass graves when the deaths began to increase after the first week. Those men were never counted.

Other astounding numbers are also included in Martin and Stephenson's work. They write:

> Only 43 percent of Americans who surrendered on Bataan are estimated to have ever returned home. Members of the 27th estimate about thirty percent, or 240, of them survived the war. Most of the more than 560 who perished were victims of the Death March, prison camps, or hell ships, including those killed when the vessels they were on were torpedoed or bombed. Only 13 men from the 27th are known to have died in

the line of duty on Luzon. Ninety from the 27th and its two attached units died at Camp O'Donnell. One hundred and ninety-nine from the 27th and its two attached units died or were murdered at the infamous Cabanatuan complex, where more than 2600 American POWs perished . . . . By comparison, about 96 percent of all Allied soldiers held as POWs in the German and Italian camps are estimated to have survived the war. [14]

Looking at those numbers for the first time, even decades later, brought me pain and memories of faces of friends—and one first cousin—who did not come home. The reunions helped, though, as we faced the past with former soldier buddies to try to find a few bright spots to talk about with a focus always on how lucky we were to have survived.

Besides talking about our journey in the Philippines and friends who did not return, a chief topic on the minds of many of us was the lifetime damage to our health as a result of our time as POWs. There had been discussions about compensation for the hardships the Philippine POWs had suffered from the numerous diseases contracted in the islands as well as the beatings and torture at the hands of the Japanese. However, so far nothing had been done on the national level, which was not surprising, knowing the speed with which bureaucracy operates.

I learned there were groups that were being pro-active and were contacting former POWs, who in turn were contacting friends or cronies they knew. One of these groups finally acquired the names of former POWs in the Pacific and was in the process of instituting action. I found it humorous, in an odd sort of way, when I learned that a great many of the population assumed that, upon our return from the Philippines, we were immediately awarded a substantial compensation for our suffering and extended medical needs.

In fact, it was not until decades later that the military (the government) finally provided the Japanese POWs a stipend. We all guessed they waited until we were all up in years; that way they wouldn't have to pay us as long. That is a sad thought to think, but it is very likely the truth. The fact still remains that we, speaking for the soldiers I knew, fought for our country as best we could, and we would do it again if necessary.

It was many years before the POWs of the Japanese were awarded some of the medals they deserved. For example, it was not until September of 1984, on Barksdale Base in Bossier City, Louisiana, that a group of us were at last awarded the Bronze Star. (See Photographs) Even more delayed was the ceremony on October 7, 2003, in Monroe, Louisiana, when I was awarded the Purple Heart. The commemoration took place in the office of United States Congressman Rodney Alexander, who submitted the required documentation many years after I was wounded on Bataan. The delay was because the doctor who operated on me to remove the shrapnel from my neck was later burned alive at the hands of the brutal Japanese; "he was doused with gasoline and set on fire,"[15] along with the entire group working with him.

Christening the *Bataan (LHD 5)*

Perhaps one of the most exciting honors for the Bataan veterans was the invitation by the United States Navy to the Christening of the *Bataan (LHD 5)* on May 18, 1996. The event was held at the Ingalls Shipbuilding complex in Pascagoula, Mississippi where the multipurpose amphibious assault ship was built. I was impressed that the Navy respected the Bataan survivors enough to allow us to invite quite a number of family members for the ceremony and a tour below deck. It was an amazing day sitting on the massive deck of that ship with my wife Demaris; my daughter Janis Pardue Hill and her husband Charles; my brother Leo Pardue, his wife Bertha and son Calvin; and my sister Iris Smith. We decided that the Navy definitely knows how to put on a celebration. (See Photographs)

In the program, which all guests received at the ceremony, was a description of the ship itself as well as the unique place the *Bataan (LHD 5)* holds among its premier vessels. A portion of the program narrative explains:

> The *LHD 5* commemorates the heroic defense of the Bataan Peninsula on the western side of Manila Bay in the Philippines, during the early days of World War II. On December 23, 1941, General Douglas MacArthur ordered his army withdrawn from Manila to the Bataan Peninsula, where Army, Navy, Marine Corps and Filipino Forces resisted an overwhelming enemy force for months, before surrendering in April 1942.

Two out of every three Americans who fought at Bataan failed to return home, having either died in battle, during the infamous 'Bataan Death March' to captivity, or in prison camps.

Veteran groups associated with the defense of Bataan and the 'Death March,' the battle for Corregidor, which fell a month after Bataan, and the aircraft carrier *USS Bataan (CVL 29)* are attending *LHD 5*'s christening ceremony.

LHD 5 is the second ship named to honor these World War II heroes. The first *Bataan* was an aircraft carrier, *CVL 29*, launched on August 1, 1943, and commissioned on November 17, 1943. *CVL 29* earned six battle stars for its World War II service in the Pacific, which included the Battle of the Philippine Sea in June 1944, and operations against the Japanese home islands, before being decommissioned in February 1947.[16]

The program also cites the principal mission of the amphibious assault ship program as being "to enable the Navy/Marine Corps team to accomplish a seamless transition from the sea to a land battle, . . ." and specifically, "to lay off a troubled area of the world, and insert forces ashore by helicopters and 50 m.p.h. LCAC hover craft."[17]

In addition, "the *LHD 5* is the Navy's first amphibious assault ship designed and built from the keel up with accommodations for female sailors."[18] Called the "Women at Sea" modification, the *LHD 5* accommodates 450 female officers, chiefs, enlisted personnel, and embarked troops. In total, the 844 foot long, 40,500-ton ship provides living spaces for 3200 crew members and troops and can travel at speeds over twenty knots.

The event and the program provided information that I had not previously known, the most striking and moving of which was that the Navy in 1943 had named and christened an earlier ship *Bataan CVL 29* to honor the defenders of Bataan. This pained me because by 1943, thousands of the Bataan defenders had perished at the hands of the cruel Japanese guards or in one of the hellish POW camps and, sadly, would never know they were honored. Similarly, we POWs still imprisoned did not know—or even ever imagine—that our sacrifices made a difference to anyone, not after the string of broken promises of planes and troops on the way, planes and troops that we actually believed would come but which never made it to the Pacific. The Japanese with its overwhelming military were victorious, and we were surrendered by our leaders; yet the Navy christened that first *Bataan* in our honor.

As I sat there on the massive *Bataan (LHD 5)*, it occurred to me that those of us who were not Navy men might never have known of the first *Bataan*, except for this second *Bataan*. And if you are not one of the "Battling Bastards of Bataan" or a family member of one, this might appear insignificant, but it is NOT. It is, in fact, of great consequence because it means to me and many others that somewhere in the hierarchy of the World War II military, some one or two or several war strategists understood the experience of soldiers sent on a mission that would be impossible to accomplish, the proverbial

"Mission Impossible." Without the planes, weaponry, supplies, and support that went to the European Theatre, we never had a chance. Those military leaders in authority, leaders with insight, believed the Battling Bastards of Bataan deserved to be appreciated for holding out—hanging on—persevering, in spite of the odds against us. And I, for one, appreciate the honor of a ship christened *Bataan*.

The return to our homeland, for some of us, had been filled with a sense of anxiety. We wondered if we might be viewed as failing to get the job done. After all, we had been surrendered. In the minds of the military decision makers, though, it was the only decision for troops who were outnumbered, starving to death, and sick with tropical diseases. We all know now it was the only decision. Of course, our leaders asked for decent treatment even though the Japanese were known for their inhumane treatment of the enemy, and they had not signed the Geneva Convention documents. To his credit, General King asked at the surrender how his soldiers would be treated, and the Japanese officer replied, "We are not barbarians." In fact, he was correct. They were worse than barbarians; they were devils.

An Angel for POWs and Veterans

Finally, one of the most rewarding experiences I have had was assisting Naline Salone, the Veterans Administration Advocate for veterans and POWs, in the planning and organization of the 50th Anniversary of the Fall of Bataan. The anniversary event was held at Barksdale in Bossier City where she was stationed.

The event was a spectacular success, largely as a result of her dedication to the Japanese POWs. I learned as I worked with her that she, and many others in the military, had a great respect for the 27th Bombardment Group and their perseverance on Bataan. She knew the details of the planes and supplies that never came and appreciated the service and the sacrifice of so many of the Army Air Corps. Naline Salone is a saint. In fact, I'm sure most POWs trusted her advice, insight, and experience more than officers of high rank. If a POW needed her assistance, the assistance was immediate. What a lady!

Final Thoughts

As I come to my story's end of my journey to the Philippines, my first thought turns to the small Bible that made the trip with me. It survived close calls, just as I had, but we made it through. I believe with every fiber of my being that the return of my Bible each time it was lost was the work of my Lord. Only God could have protected that Bible from the bomb that destroyed everything around it. I also believe, without a doubt, the faith secured from God's Holy Word lifted me up through the difficult and often desperate times. God and my faith saw me through the storms during those four and a half years in the Philippines. I treasure that little Bible and will pass it on to my family when God calls me home.

My next thought centers on my soldier friends and my cousin who didn't make it back, what they suffered, and how they passed from this life to the next under the most dreadful and heartbreaking conditions. There was no reason that they should have died the way they did. To witness one's fellow man suffer and to be unable to fix it and make it right is a pain like no other. Then, you're forced to bury them, without family, without a headstone, in a foreign land on the other side of the world. That is the haunting tragedy that lives within those of us who were able to survive.

And my final thought relates to my country, its citizens and its leaders, who must protect it from those who would destroy it if they could. There will always be an emperor, a dictator, or a president somewhere in the world who will seek to bring down or take over the United States of America. If I could instill one facet of my Philippine experience into the minds and hearts of the youth of today, it would be the feeling of horror when you realize that you no longer have a say in anything or in any aspect of your lives. You are <u>nothing</u>, and you are <u>dispensable</u>.

Only in America do we enjoy the freedoms so many other people of the world are denied. The younger generation holds the future in their hands, and they must ensure that our freedoms continue for their children and their children and their children. I hope that they will seek peace and be kind. Jesus speaks of peace in the seventh of His Beatitudes: "Blessed are the peacemakers for they shall be called sons of God" (Matthew 5:9, KJV).

Once, in conversation with an individual who wanted to know, in a few words, what I thought the Bible was about, I immediately said, "It's a book about love." Those who love seek peace; those who seek peace love others.

I have known hate. Love is better.

EPILOGUE

J.C. Pardue—my father—POW #1000, passed away on June 25, 2012, at the age of 94. He was buried with full military honors, with his wife of 65 years there to accept the flag that draped his coffin.

Technical Sergeant J.C. Pardue survived atrocities no human should face—on the Bataan Death March, in POW camps, and as a slave in Japan. He survived dehydration, malnutrition, tropical diseases and fevers of every sort, torture, and beatings. And he survived the haunting memories that must have plagued him for years. He survived and lived a long and happy Christian life, content to the end that his God, his Bible, and his faith had seen him through.

And J.C. Pardue was not the only victim of the barbaric, animalistic Japanese guards. He was one of thousands who never gave up, who mourned their fellow soldiers when they were forced to bury them but who continued to hang on.

They stand as representatives of the best America has to offer. Accurately labeled "The Greatest Generation," without them, the United States of America would look very different today.

As I come to the end of my journey through my father's past via the myriad of pages he wrote, I share some words from the newspaper article, published after his funeral in his city's newspaper:

> Journalist Scott Rogers interviewed Tommy Sims, the Northeastern Louisiana Department of Veterans Affairs, with whom my dad often visited, sharing stories and even copies of some of the drawings from fellow POWs. The drawings were most often of the guards who tortured and beat them, guards that would have shot them if they had found the drawings.[19]

At the end of the article, Sims summarized POW #1000, our family's beloved patriarch, as follows:

> I know this sounds cliché, but he definitely was a patriot and a great American. He suffered a whole lot under the hands of the Japanese government. It was pretty awful. Even going through all that – tortured, beaten, and starved and treated as bad as a human could be treated – he always had a positive attitude. He was an inspiration. I am very sorry we lost a great American.

He was a great example of "The Greatest Generation." We're losing them quickly, and it won't be too much longer until they're all gone.[20]

But my father and all the other patriot heroes never considered themselves heroes. They just did what had to be done.

Assignment Complete

As I approached the end of the project that I had promised my dad I would accomplish for him, I was swamped by a myriad of varied, unexpected emotions. I had presumed I would feel great relief, satisfaction, and joy that the task was done to the best of my ability and that my promise to my beloved father had been fulfilled. And I did, of course, experience those feelings, grateful that after many long days and nights, the text was nearly ready for publication. I had attained my primary goal: *honor my father as well as others who persevered through the barbaric, atrocious treatment as POWs of the Japanese.*

What I did not anticipate was the great sadness—the sorrow—which consumed me and overshadowed the joy. This I had not expected, nor did I immediately understand it. Then I realized I had never known the extent of the suffering my father and the other POWs had endured. It shatters for a bit one's confidence in humankind. When there is no kindness, terror reigns; and that someone I have loved since my childhood had faced that terror was devastating.

It was difficult—at times, physically painful—to learn the details of the Bataan Death March, the prison camps, and the Hell Ships. However, my father had survived, unlike thousands. Not only that, he prospered, returning home and living to the age of ninety-four, in spite of the maladies he continued to suffer after his return home. He was loved and respected, as were all those men who hung on and persevered. He even recovered enough to talk to many young people, including two of his grandchildren, who were researching the event for their history projects.

Besides his faith and love of God, the other trait I admired in my father was his kindness; he was one of the kindest men I have ever known. What I have always found most worthy of praise about his kind manner is that in all the years when I lived at home—growing up, high school, college—I never heard him say a profane word about his Japanese guards. By this, I mean he described their actions, and what they did was in most cases barbaric; but he never expressed anger or a desire for revenge. I never heard him use words unacceptable in polite conversation. He just did not do that. I find that amazing.

I close with a warning from Lord Acton: "Power corrupts and absolute power corrupts absolutely," found at the beginning of Orwell's great novel *1984*.[21] My civilized, kind, and loving father and his fellow soldiers had suffered because of the age-old condition Lord Acton described.

It is a part of the history of the world, and it will happen again. Indeed, it's taking place in our world today, even as I have sat and transcribed the words of my POW father. These members of "The Greatest Generation" suffered almost beyond our comprehension so that their children and their children's children could enjoy the freedom not present in so many places. We must keep their history alive.

—Janis Pardue Hill, PhD

APPENDIX 1

Timeline
October 29, 1939 - July 13, 1949

(Bolded dates refer to my personal timeline dates.)

1939-1941

October 29, 1939	**I enlist in the United States Army Air Corps at Barksdale Air Force Base, Bossier City, Louisiana.**
November, 1939-Summer-1941	**I trained at three bases: Barksdale Air Force Base in Bossier City, Scott Field in Illinois, and Hunter Field in Savannah, Georgia.**
August 15-September 28, 1941	My group, the US Air Force 27th Bombardment Group, participates in the Louisiana Maneuvers.
November 7, 1941	The 27th embarks to Manilla, Philippines, from San Francisco, California, on the USS *Coolidge*.

November 20, 1941	We arrive in Manila, Philippines and board trucks for Fort McKinley.
December 7, 1941	The Japanese attack Pearl Harbor.
December 7, 1941	Ten hours later, the Japanese attack the Philippines and other islands held by American forces.
December 22, 1941	Japanese forces invade Luzon and in a short time enter Manila and take control of the capital city.
December 24, 1941	**On orders from General MacArthur, American and Philippine Troops retreat to the peninsula of Bataan on an interisland steamer.**
December 24, 1941	General Macarthur, along with Philippine President Quezon, retreats to Corregidor to command from the island fortress.
December 25, 1941	**We arrive at the Bataan Peninsula and go ashore on Christmas Day; we begin journey north to the middle of Luzon Island.**
Circa January 2, 1941	**We establish a line and begin to fortify ourselves halfway up the island.**

1942

January– April 7, 1942	**We hold the island with little food and equipment, enduring countless attacks from the Japanese bombers and Japanese infantry.**
March 11, 1942	General Macarthur, on the orders of President Franklin Roosevelt, departs Corregidor with his family and staff in the middle of the night and relocates to Australia, making his famous promise, **"I will return."**
April 1-7, 1942	The Japanese assaults increase and we begin to hear rumors of a possible surrender.

April 8-9, 1942	General King makes the decision to surrender (against the will of General MacArthur). General King surrenders to General Nagano Kamaechiro and Colonel Nakayama Matoo at12:30 p.m. on April 9, 1942.
April 10, 1942	**We begin the infamous Bataan Death March. It begins from the tip of the Bataan Peninsula as well as other positions along the route. Many prisoners are taken as the Japanese encounter them along the route. An estimated 6000 American and Filipinos die from starvation, disease, or execution by the Japanese guards.**
Circa April 14-17, 1942	**As American Prisoners of War, those of us who survive the death march arrive at O'Donnell POW Camp and immediately suffer harsh treatment from brutal guards in addition to a lack of food, water, and medical treatment.**
April 18, 1942	Allied Forces establish the Southwest Pacific Headquarters in Australia. This area includes the Philippines. General Douglas MacArthur is named Commander-in-Chief of the Southwest Pacific Area (SWPA).
July 4, 1942	**I am transferred with other POWs healthy enough to make the move to Camp Cabantuan where conditions are somewhat improved.**

1943

February 1943	General MacArthur reorganizes his former headquarters in the Philippines; it becomes the new US Army Forces in the Far East.
January–December, 1943	**I remain in Camp Cabanatuan until I am one of about 1600 other POWs selected to go to Japan and work as a slave in the Yawata Steel Factory.**

1944

July 17, 1944	**We are boarded onto one of the infamous Hell Ships, the *Nissyo Maru*, to make the journey to Japan.**
August 4, 1944	**I arrive at Fukuoka Camp Number 3 and begin working at the Yahatta Steel Mill where I work as a slave until the atomic bomb is dropped on Nagasaki, which is about one year and four days later.**
October 20, 1944	US forces successfully land on east coast beaches of Leyte as part of the Allied invasion of Leyte and on a radio broadcast, General MacArthur announces, ""**People of the Philippines, I have returned!**" Many Americans today are not aware that this day is known as A-Day (Assault Day).
December 1944	General MacArthur announces the end of organized Japanese resistance on Leyte. Japanese defenders continue to fight until December 31, and some disorganized resistance continues through May 1945.

1945

January 1945	General Macarthur leads his forces in the invasion of Luzon.
April 6, 1945	A reorganization brings the Southwest Pacific Army under the new command of Army Forces Pacific, led by General MacArthur.
May 8, 1945	V-E Day (Victory in Europe Day) Nazi Germany surrenders to the Allies, ending the war in Europe.
Midnight June 30 - July 1, 1945	Luzon Campaign ends officially. The campaign in Mindanao continues until the end of the war.
August 6, 1945	The US drops an atomic bomb on Hiroshima, Japan.
August 9, 1945	The US drops an atomic bomb on Nagasaki, Japan.
August 9, 1945	Many Japanese guards of prison camps flee. Others begin to execute POWs in their charge.
August 15, 1945	V-J Day (Victory over Japan Day) or V-P Day (Victory in the Pacific Day). Japan surrenders, ending World War II. The news reaches the US on August 14, 1945, as a result of time zone differences.
August 30- September 30, 1945	United States military drops supplies and messages to POWs stranded in camps in the Pacific to begin liberation of POWs in the prison camps.
August 15- September 12, 1945	**Two friends and I leave camp through the Fukuoka POW Camp back gate and hitchhike/ find train to the southern end of Kyshu Island to connect with American forces.**

September 2, 1945	General Douglas MacArthur signs Peace Treaty with Japan on the deck of the USS *Missouri* (Japanese Envoys were Foreign Minister Mamora Shigemitsu and Gen. Yoshijiro Umezu.)
September 13, 1945	I depart Japan for Manila where I am transferred to a Depot for Repatriation.
September 25, 1945	I depart Manila for the United States.
October 20, 1945	I arrive in San Francisco, California, and I am sent to Letterman Hospital.
November, 1945	I return home to Union Parish in Louisiana and stay with my family for the remainder of my leave. I report to Barksdale AFB to finish out my tour of duty.

1946-1949

May 1, 1946	I marry and begin family life.
August, 1946	I am sent to the hospital at Fort Sam Houston in Texas where I am treated for a variety of conditions.
August 6, 1946	I am honorably discharged while at Fort Sam Houston.
August 7, 1946	After my Honorable Discharge on August 6, 1946, I re-enlist for three more years.
July 13, 1949	I am honorably discharged for a second time and return to the life of a civilian patriot.

APPENDIX 2

Japanese Prison Camps

Akenobe #6	Batavia, Java
Beppu	**Bilibid Prison**
Bridge House Jail, China	Burma
Cabanatuan #1	Cabanatuan #3
Camp O'Donnell	Changi, Singapore
D-12, Hitachi	Davao Penal Colony
Fengtai, China	Fukuoka #1
Fukuoka #2	**Fukuoka #3**
Fukuoka #10	Fukuoka #11
Fukuoka #17	Fukuoka #22
Hakodate Branch Camp #2	Hoten, Mukden, Manchuria
Initial Phase – Philippines	Jinsen, Korea
Kiangwan, China	Manila, Port Area
Matsushima, Tokyo Camp #2-D	Makaishima, Honshu
Mukden, Manchuria (temporary)	Nakhon Pathom, Thailand
Naval POW Camp, Shanghai	Notogawa #9-B
October Ship (Hellship)	Omine

Osaka #3, Oeyama	Osaka #5-B
Osaka #12-B	Osaka Group, Sakurajima, Osaka
Palawan Barracks	Rangoon Prison, Burma
Roku Roshi	Saigon POW Camp, French Indo-China
Sendai Camp #6, Hanawa	Sendai Camp #11 Southeast Asia – Saigon, Port Area
SS Oryuku Maru (Hellship)	Sumatra
Thailand (Siam)	Tientsin, China
Umeda Bonshu	Utashinai, Hokkaido
War Road Jail, Shanghai, China	Woosung
Zentsuji Headquarters	Taiwan Formosa (includes Camps 31, Taihoku; Camp V, Taihoku; Camp VI, Taihoku; Kinkaseki, Camp II, Taichu; Camp III, Heito; Camp IV, Kagi & Takao)

(This is a partial list of the more well-known POW camps in Japan. In total there were more than eighty Japanese prison camps.)

APPENDIX 3

The Japanese Manifesto

Japan will use whatever powers that it has to conquer the United States, England and the Jews. The Japanese Military Forces will be used in the first round of struggle against the American Imperialist, then other methods will be constructed until Nippon takes over the American Homeland and the Jews. A Greater East Asia Co-Prosperity Sphere will be established to give World prosperity in the future. Japan will never give up until America is conquered.

Captured American Prisoners of War will be punished according to the Japanese Military Code of Warfare and as Japan sees fit.

Taken from:
The *U.S. Infantry Journal* 1944
"Through The Eyes of The Japanese"
(United States Infantry Association, 1944)

APPENDIX 4

Declaration of War Speech by President Franklin Roosevelt, December 8, 1941.

Mr. Vice President, Mr. Speaker, Members of the Senate, and of the House of Representatives:

Yesterday, December 7th, 1941 – a date which will live in infamy – the United States of America was suddenly and deliberately attacked by naval and air forces of the Empire of Japan.

The United States was at peace with that nation and, at the solicitation of Japan, was still in conversation with its government and its emperor looking toward the maintenance of peace in the Pacific.

Indeed, one hour after Japanese air squadrons had commenced bombing in the American island of Oahu, the Japanese ambassador to the United States and his colleague delivered to our Secretary of State a formal reply to a recent American message. And while this reply stated that it seemed useless to continue the existing diplomatic negotiations, it contained no threat or hint of war or of armed attack.

It will be recorded that the distance of Hawaii from Japan makes it obvious that the attack was deliberately planned many days or even weeks ago. During the intervening time, the Japanese government has deliberately sought to deceive the United States by false statements and expressions of hope for continued peace.

The attack yesterday on the Hawaiian Islands has caused severe damage to American naval and military forces. I regret to tell you that very many American lives have been lost. In addition, American ships have been reported torpedoed on the high seas between San Francisco and Honolulu.

Yesterday, the Japanese government also launched an attack against Malaya.

Last night, Japanese forces attacked Hong Kong.

Last night, Japanese forces attacked Guam.

Last night, Japanese forces attacked the Philippine Islands.

Last night, the Japanese attacked Wake Island.

And this morning, the Japanese attacked Midway Island.

Japan has, therefore, undertaken a surprise offensive extending throughout the Pacific area. The facts of yesterday and today speak for themselves. The people of the United States have already formed their opinions and well understand the implications to the very life and safety of our nation.

As Commander in Chief of the Army and Navy, I have directed that all measures be taken for our defense. But always will our whole nation remember the character of the onslaught against us.

No matter how long it may take us to overcome this premeditated invasion, the American people in their righteous might will win through to absolute victory.

I believe that I interpret the will of the Congress and of the people when I assert that we will not only defend ourselves to the uttermost, but will make it very certain that this form of treachery shall never again endanger us.

Hostilities exist. There is no blinking at the fact that our people, our territory, and our interests are in grave danger.

With confidence in our armed forces, with the unbounding determination of our people, we will gain the inevitable triumph – so help us God.

I ask that the Congress declare that since the unprovoked and dastardly attack by Japan on Sunday, December 7th, 1941, a state of war has existed between the United States and the Japanese empire.

APPENDIX 5

Orientation for Recovered Personnel

Note from editor: I found this little booklet in my father's papers. **My dad kept everything!** It was obviously given to him at the 29th Replacement Depot in Manila where POWs were processed. I was amazed that he had kept his personal copy of this document and that it was in such good shape, except for the discoloration of the pages. Because the booklet contained so much information disseminated to the returning soldiers, I found it provided much insight into the process of repatriation and, actually, gave me a picture of the days spent at the Depot. Thus, I reproduced it, below, for your perusal. (See Photo of Parts of Booklet in Photographs)

INTRODUCTORY MEMO:

Headquarters
29TH REPLACEMENT DEPOT
APO 238

Mm/aag

1 September 1945

SUBJECT: Welcome To The 29th Replacement Depot

TO: Personnel Arriving From War Zones

1. As commanding officer, I welcome you to the 29th Replacement Depot. It is my personal desire and the desire of all members of the Depot staff and others associated with us, to your stay here as pleasant as possible.

2. In the succeeding pages of this booklet, we have tried to outline briefly for you the program which is planned and the facilities which we are able to offer during your stay with us. There is established an information service in each area which is designed to answer other questions which we have not been able to anticipate.

3. The personnel of this Depot are at your service on a twenty-four hour schedule.

4. Good luck and a speedy trip home!

MARTIN MOSHBERGER
Colonel, FA Commanding

ORIENTATION FOR RECOVERED PERSONNEL

Your Company

Upon arrival at the 29th Replacement Depot, you were assigned to the company in which you are presently located. You should already have received a ditty bag from the American Red Cross which contains the minimum essential items for your immediate physical comfort. In addition, you should already have had your first meal and are now in a position to consider what comes next.

This we are attempting to tell you in this booklet, particularly insofar as procedure in the 29th Replacement Depot is concerned. For further orientation, you should also have received a copy of the pamphlet "Where Do We Go From Here?" (War Department # 21-28).

During the next few hours, you will receive your issue of clothing, and the American Red Cross will contact you with reference to the information necessary to set up the locator system which will enable you to receive mail and packages which have already arrived in Manila, and which will enable the Red Cross to answer questions of your friends and relatives with respect to your arrival. Otherwise, your time is your own. Use it insofar as possible to get rest and relaxation because during the next 36-48 hours following this brief rest period, your program is going to be rather strenuous.

The Physical Examination

For all American military personnel, a complete physical examination to include immunizations and dental surveys will be made. A non-commissioned officer from your company has your group time schedule and will conduct your group to the dispensary where the examinations will take place.

Civilian personnel will receive a modified examination but will report to the dispensary in the same manner as military personnel.

Dental and Dispensary Services

Whenever you are in need of emergency dental or dispensary services, make application at the orderly room and you will be given the necessary information for reporting to the Depot dental clinic or your own dispensary.

Interviews and Questionnaires

After the completion of the physical examination, your non-commissioned officer will conduct you to Depot Headquarters where an interviewing team will assist you in filling out all the necessary forms and questionnaires which pertain to your activities since you left military control. These forms will be the basic for the preparation of a new service record and allied papers. For civilian personnel, no military records are prepared, but specified forms and questionnaires are completed.

There are several questionnaires which are required in each case, and this process is likely to be rather tiresome; every effort will be made, however, to complete the work as rapidly as possible.

Pay

As soon as the necessary information is received from GHQ AFPAC, rolls will be prepared and sent to your company for signature. (Only American military personnel and civilian employees of the War department will be paid by this Headquarters. The Navy and the Dutch Government will pay their personnel.)

War Department instructions provide that you will receive a partial pay equal to three months of the pay due you according to your last verified grade. The purpose of the pay is to give you some cash for immediate needs. The Office of Special Settlement Accounts in New York will be furnished the necessary information for the computation of all pay due you while in absent status on the basis of the affidavits which you make during the process of completing all questionnaires, and any other available War Department records.

The following instruction is taken from Circular No. 19, par 5c, General Headquarters, United States Army Forces, Pacific, dated 9 July 1945, and should be carefully noted:

"Each individual will be instructed that only one such partial payment is authorized; that his pay account will be settled by the Office of Special Settlement Accounts, 27 Pine Street, New York, N. Y., and that he will not submit a pay voucher or sign a payroll covering any period of his absence from controllable jurisdiction except for settlement made by that office."

This means that no more back pay will be paid on any regular pay roll; your current pay, however, begins to accrue effective with the date on which you returned to military control.

<u>Red Cross</u>

The American Red Cross has increased its personnel and facilities in order to give you the very best service possible. You are invited to contact the Red Cross representative in your company, in your battalion, and the Red Cross Director's office which is located at Depot Headquarters. These people are available to give you the services for which the Red Cross is famous. Be sure to locate the Service Center serving your battalion. Here you will find the Red Cross Canteen, and the lounge rooms.

The Red Cross will make monetary grants to those who have need of them upon individual application.

<u>Service Center</u>

The Service Centers are organized for the purpose of rendering you the personal services which are available at the Depot. Included in the centers are the Red Cross lounges and canteens mentioned above, the Post Exchanges, where all items are free, and the Information and Education Section where you can obtain reading materials of various kinds, including books, magazines, and newspapers. There is also an officer available to answer any questions you may have. If he is unable to answer your questions, he will refer your question to the Depot sections where the answers are most likely to be available.

Cable Messages

You may send cable messages from this center. Messages will be accepted at the center and transmitted hourly on teletype from Depot Headquarters to Press wireless. Information as to rates and censorship will be available here.

Mail

All personnel, civilian, and military will use the following return address:

> Name
> Liberated Personnel Section
> APO 501, c/o Postmaster
> San Francisco, California

Incoming mail will be delivered to you in your company.

Outgoing mail will be censored by Base Censor, APO 75, and be transported to the United States by air transportation through Army Postal Service. If you desire air service in the interior to the United States, you should add the air mail stamps.

Air mail rates anywhere where the United States Postal System is in operation are: 6 cents per ½ oz; Canada 8 cents per oz. Civilian addresses in Europe 30 cents per ½ oz; Australia 5 cents per oz., 5 cents additional for air inside Australia.

The directory for all personnel will be maintained at APO 238. Incoming WD Cables and mail will be delivered by courier from GHQ to APO 238 for delivery.

Information And Education Section

In the Information and Education Section of the Service Centers, you will find a roster of personnel assigned to the Depot. This roster is compiled by places of residence in the event you are interested in looking up people from your home state.

In addition to those rosters, the Service Center will maintain a complete set of rosters of incoming personnel which you may check at any time for friends or relatives.

If you have relatives in the Manila area, you may inform the officer at the Information and Education Section and every effort possible will be made to arrange contacts with them.

Religious Services

The services of the Chaplain at the Depot will include worship services, spiritual consultations, personal interviews and visits.

Three Chaplain's offices are available. The first is the Main Chapel located near the 61st Battalion; the second is located between the 59th and 60th Battalions, and the third is located between the 61st and 62nd Battalions. In each office, there is available a Protestant and Catholic chaplain.

Worship services will be held in the Main Chapel on Sundays and also in the battalion areas, at places and on schedules to be announced.

Chaplain Jacob Levy of the 5th Replacement Depot will hold services in the Depot chapels on Wednesdays and Fridays and will, by appointment, make personal visits.

Mormon services will be held in the Depot Chapel each week on schedules to be announced later.

Athletic and Recreation Program

Active sports such as baseball and boxing will be presented by teams composed of operational personnel.

Volleyball, horseshoe, and other games in which you may participate will be available in your company. Indoor games are in the Service Center.

Movies will be presented nightly, and USO and local shows will be announced periodically. The 86th and 227th Army Ground Forces bands and a locally organized dance band are available for entertainment as scheduled.

Awards, Decorations, and Service Stripes

As soon as possible after your arrival at the Depot, your records will be checked to determine what awards, decorations, and service stripes you are entitled to. These will be issued to you as soon as possible. Be sure to give full information with respect to these things when you fill out the affidavits during the processing period.

Laundry Service

Laundry services are available. Laundry will be picked up and delivered according to schedules which will be announced in your company and posted on the bulletin boards.

Alteration of Clothing

If your clothes need altering, you will find a tailoring shop located in your area.

Fruit Vendors

Native fruits are available in fruit vending tents on the post and in various fruit shops along the highway. It is recommended that you do not purchase this fruit owing to the health hazard, but if you do, be sure that it is properly washed. Fruits with skin breaks should be avoided because of possible contamination.

Hair Cuts

If you need a haircut, you will find a barber shop in your company. Haircuts are free.

The Depot

The 29th Replacement Depot was activated on 1 July 1945. It is composed of four battalions of four companies each. It is located on the Manila-Santa Rosa Highway in the province of Rizal approximately eighteen miles south of Manila.

The primary mission of the Depot has been to forward replacements to the fighting units from the United States. Our primary mission now is to return you as quickly as possible to the United States.

The Philippines And The Filipinos

You probably already have some very good general ideas about the Philippines and the Filipino people. There are a few things, however, that we should like to emphasize at this camp. The Filipinos have been extremely helpful to the American forces in the reconquest of the islands, and we have their good will and admiration. We want to retain that.

You will find the people are extremely courteous and friendly. Civilians, however, are not permitted in the camp areas without a pass, so don't expect to have them visit you in camp except by special permission from your battalion headquarters.

Philippine currency is in units of pesos and centavos; one peso is worth 50 cents, and one centavo is equal to one-half cent in American money. A caution: In the Philippines, there are several types of currency in circulation which are not valid and which will not be acceptable at the Finance Office, Post Exchange, or at Army Post Offices. Only Philippine Treasury Certificates (pre-war issue) and Philippine Victory Currency are lawful. Coins are acceptable provided that they have not been severely mutilated. Two tests of validity of bills are: (1) Do the words "Treasury Certificate" appear on the bill; and (2) Is the bill printed on regular American currency paper containing red and blue threads. The following types of currency are not lawful money:

> Philippine National Bank Notes
> Philippine Emergency Currency
> Guerilla Notes
> Japanese Currency
> Japanese Invasion Currency
> Chinese Currency

War Crimes Information

In view of the fact that information concerning "War Crimes" is at the present time highly classified, you must, under no circumstances, divulge any information having to do with this subject to any person except those who have direct authorization from the intelligence section, this Depot. This applies especially to secret prison camp organization and escape or invasion plans. Information on this subject, which is called for on the forms to be filled out upon entering the Depot is authorized. In the event that interviews concerning this subject are necessary, the persons conducting these interviews will have the necessary authorization, and prior to their receiving the information, must identify themselves by the presentation of proper credentials.

Leaves and Passes

Your processing is not complete until you have been paid and, except under exceptional circumstances, you must not leave the post for more than short periods of time until all processing is complete.

The control section will report your name to your company when you have been cleared through all steps of the processing. If it is important that you leave the post before processing is complete, make application at your company orderly room. Every request will be decided on its merits.

Changes

Should change in the procedure become necessary, prompt notification will be given.

Free Message To Your Next of Kin

If you receive a message from your next of kin in the United States, you may reply to this message, at government expense as follows:

a. 25 words to include the address and your signature may be sent.

b. Do not use the name and address of the person to whom you are sending the message. You will notice that the message you received is preceded by a number and the symbol "REPAT." In replying, you should address your message as follows:

(1) If you are a civilian, use the symbol "PIWAR," preceded by the same number which preceded the symbol "REPAT" in the message you received.

(2) If you belong to the armed forces of the United States, use the symbol "SPXPC-M" preceded by the same number which preceded the symbol "REPAT" in the message you received.

(3) For example – if you received a message beginning with "77REPAT," your reply should be addressed to "77PIWAR" (civilian) or 77SPXPC-M" (military).

(4) No other address may be used. This leaves you 23 words, including your signature, that you may send in replay.

Blank forms for reply are available at the orderly room of your company.

These forms will be collected at your company and transmitted from Manila.

APPENDIX 6

Document: Letterman General Hospital

Army Ground Forces Liaison Office

ARMY GROUND FORCES LIAISON OFFICE
CRISSY FIELD ANNEX
LETTERMAN GENERAL HOSPITAL
SAN FRANCISCO, CALIFORNIA

TO: Liberated Prisoners of War

May we take this opportunity to welcome you in behalf of General Devers, Commanding General, Army Ground Forces?

The Commanding General of Army Ground Forces is vitally interested in your welfare, and this Liaison Office has been established for the primary purpose of assisting you in any problems or questions that may, or will, arise during your stay in this, or any hospital to which you may be sent for further treatment.

What branches constitute Army Ground Forces? Infantry, Artillery, (Coast, Field, or Anti-Aircraft), Tank Destroyers, Armored Forces, Calvary, and all service units which service an army headquarters or subordinate units (division corps etc.)

Generally speaking, your stay at this hospital will be short and pleasant, and if you do not find time to visit your Army Ground Forces Liaison Office, make a mental note to see your Army Ground Forces Liaison Office in the hospital to which you may be sent in a few days.

You will want to enjoy your stay at home to the utmost, and you will, IF you are sure that when you go home on leave all personal problems, such as your promotion, authorized ribbons and decorations, the procedure you will go through between now and reassignment or separation, things you should know and do while on furlough, and any other matter of major importance to you are taken care of beforehand.

Your Army Ground Forces Liaison Office is located in the Administration Building, or phone 4451.

EDGAR FORD,
Captain, Infantry,
Army Ground Forces, Liaison Officer

APPENDIX 7

Former POW Medical History

Please type or print your answers in ink.

A. Identifying Data: Date: X /XX /XX

Pardue,	**J. C.**	**(F.N.I.O.)**
Last Name	**First Name**	

1. Social Security Number   **xxx-xx-xxxx**
2. VA Claim Number   **C-xx xxx xxx.**
3. Last Military Identification Number   **x xxx xxx.**
4. Present Age **xx**   Age on Capture **24**   Years **7** Months
   Age on Release From Captivity **27**   Years **10** Months
   Age on Discharge From Active Military Service **31**
5. Date of Induction Into Military Service **October 20, 1939**
6. Active Military Service (Circle all Applicable): **Army** Navy
   Air Force Marine Corps Coast Guard Other (Specify)

7. Grade and Service:
	Grade	Service
At Time of Induction	**Pvt.**	**Army Air Corps**
At Time of Capture	**Sgt.**	**U. S. Infantry**
At Time of Release from Captivity	**Sgt.**	**U. S. Infantry**
At Time of Military Discharge	**T/Sgt.**	**U. S. Air Force**

8. Prisoner of War Category (Circle all Applicable): WWI
   WWII (Europe)   **WWII (Pacific)**   Korea
   Vietnam   Other (Specify)

9. Theaters Or Theaters In Which You Participated:
   Europe   Pacific   China, Burma, India
   Korea   Southeast Asia
   Other (Specify) Japan & Philippine Islands

10. Name Of Country Or Countries In Which You Were A Prisoner:
    Philippine Islands and Japan

11. Date Of Military Discharge: **July 13, 1949**

12. Type Of Military Discharge (Specify) **Honorable –**
    AR 615-361Certificate of
    Disability for Discharge

13. Marital Status:
At Time of Entrance Into The Service	**Single**
At Time of Capture	**Single**
At Time of Repatriation	**Single**
At Present	**Married**

B. History of Captivity:

1. Approximate Date of Capture: **April 9, 1942**
2. Circumstances Of Capture:
   (Check The Items Or Questions That Apply)

In A Battle _____ During Isolation Of Your Unit _____ During Isolation

From Your Unit _____ During An Advance _____ During A Retreat _____

Shot Down In An Aircraft _____

Ordered To Surrender By A Higher U.S. Or Allied Authority **YES**

Other _____

Were You Captured Alone? **NO**

Were You Captured In A Group? **YES**

If so, How Large Was The Group? **100** Did The Group Remain Intact During Captivity? **NO** How Many Of Your Original Group Survived Captivity? **30% Est.** Were You Injured At The Time Of Captivity? **YES**

If So, How Were You Injured? Describe Your Injury

"2 days earlier, after an enemy mortar attack, a number of shells had fallen near-by, I was scrambling for cover; after this I got up & noticed that the skin on top of both my hands was torn off, wide sections were bleeding, they were put in bandages after this."

3.   What Type Of Work Did You Do While In Captivity? (Check The Questions That Apply)

Farm Worker **X** Factory Worker **X** Construction Worker **X** Miner __

(Specify) ___Dock Worker ___Other (Specify) ___None __

Year 1944, farm work at Camp Cabantuan, alternating 50% of time to build (moving dirt) construction of enemy airplane landing strip that was about two (2) miles from the camp in the Philippine Islands. While in Japan, mid-1944 to end of war, I worked at a large steel factory doing a variety of jobs – hard labor moving material & brick 50% of time, other times helping with steel mill repairs, also shoveling cinders from the coal de-gasification units.

4. Escape:
   Did You Participate In A Plan To Escape? **YES** Did You Make An Active Attempt To Escape? **YES** If So, Were You Successful? **NO**
5. Length Of Captivity In Months: **42**
6. Names Of Prison (s): **POW Camp O'Donnell; POW Camp Cabanatuan #1; Old Bilibid Prison (In Manila); and Fukuoka #3 in Japan** Do Not Know __
7. Location Of Prison(s): **Camp O'Donnell is located in Tarlac Province, Philippines; Camp Cabanatuan #1, located in Nueva Ecija Province (central plains) Luzon Island, Philippines; Old Bilibid Prison is in Manila, Rizal Province, in the Philippine Islands; Fukuoka #3 POW Camp is located in the Northernmost part on the Island of Kyushu – Kyushu is the Southern one of the three (3) large and main islands of Japan.**
8. Experience During Capture: (Answer "Yes" or "No")

		Number of Times	Number of Days
a.	Intimidation **YES**	**Daily**	**about 1200**
b.	Beatings **YES**	**3 beatings, about 50 clubbings**	**about 50**
c.	Witness Beatings **YES**	**2000**	**600 about 50% of time**
d.	Physical Torture **YES**	**100**	**100**
e.	Witness Physical Torture **YES**	**1000**	**600 about 50% of time**

Our physician, Dr. "M," belonging to my organization, the 17th, was executed with others (139 massacred) on an airfield construction project – gasoline was thrown on them, then with a lighted match they were set afire; some died of gunfire.

f. Psychological Torture ("Brainwashing")   **YES**   **50**   **50**

g. Were attempts made to use you for propaganda purposes?
   YES   No   **12**

h. Isolation in Close Quarters   **YES**

(1) Prison Ships **YES** Number of Days **17-day voyage to Japan in July and August 1944**

(2) Attacked Prison Ships **YES**   Number of Times **3 times**

(3) Railroad Box Cars **YES** Number of Days **One Day/ one night**

(4) Attacked Box Cars **NO** Number of Times _____

(5) Solitary Confinement **NO**   Number of Days _____

i. Forced Marches **YES**   Number of Days **10**

j. Attacked Forced Marches **YES**   Number of Times **15 est.**

k. Prolonged Periods of Fear And Anxiety **YES**   No _____

l. Prolonged Periods of Depression   **YES**   No _____

m. Prolonged Periods of Feeling of Helplessness **YES** No _____

n. Loneliness and Isolation From Other POWs **YES** No _____

o. Unable to Function Or Work Because of Psychological or Emotional

Stress **YES**   Explain:

Stress factor mainly caused by the helplessness, physical weakness and poor health, there were small amounts of food to eat –mainly rice; all of my relatives and friends died near the first, then when I made new friends they also soon died.

* p. Thoughts of Suicide **NEVER**   Number of Times _____

Many times the enemy guards suggested and kept after me – several (myself also others) that I should commit "Hari Kiri," by cutting my stomach open with a knife – their so called and acclaimed heroicstyle. I resented the idea of having to listen to their pagan brainwash and gestures of heathenism – their cheapening mind-control methods.

q. Attempts at Suicide **NO**   Number of Times _____

r. Other: _____

197

9. Would You Be Willing To Discuss With The Interviewing Medical Examiner Your Relationship With Your Fellow POWs? Yes **X** No ____

I have acquired numbers of photographs taken in two POW camps where I was located, the places I stayed, slept on the floor, the buildings, the morgue, crematorium and surroundings, the photos have also been developed into a slide-show for an accurate account of our life style and the circumstances.

10. Did You Have Periods Of Nightmares, Confusion, Or Delirium During Captivity? **Yes X** No ____

Nightmares came after repatriation, but none during the time while in POW camps that I remember, those were times of confusion and times of exhaustion.

11. Wounds and Injuries During Captivity: None ___ **Head X Chest X** Abdomen ___ Back ___ Arms ___ Legs ___ Other **Hands X**

12. Exposure to Cold: Before Capture – **None X**

Frostbite __ Trench Foot __

Cold Water Immersion Foot or Hand __ Other __

In Captivity – None __ Frostbite __ Trench Foot __

Cold Water Immersion Foot or Hand __ **Other X**

Often required to stand outside during cold winter nights and we were forced to take calisthenics while bareheaded and barefooted for four (4) and sometimes six (6) hours – sometimes it was just stand in the cold – requirement 2 or 3 times a week.

Exposure to Heat: Before Capture – **None X** Heat Exhaustion __

Heat Stroke __ Loss of Consciousness __

Frequency __ Times Per Day __

In Captivity – None __ **Heat Exhaustion YES**

Heat Stroke __ Loss of Consciousness **X**

Frequency **X** Times Per Day **1**

13. Radiation Exposure: (Not applicable unless specifically explained) **I was located in an area near Nagasaki after the second "A" bomb, was exposed to radioactive fall-out – developed fevers and upset stomach.**

14. Did You Receive News From Home? **Yes a couple of letters** No ____
How Often? Occasionally ____ Rarely **X** Never ____
Was This A Significant Factor? Yes ____ No X **Not really, we knew the enemy was shielding their failing efforts.**

15. Dietary History: Estimate Weight On Entering The Service **?**
Perhaps 130-135 pounds
Estimate Lowest Weight In Captivity **80s** Pounds **(Just estimated somewhere in the 80s)**
Present weight **135** Pounds **More so, my weight falls into a range pattern, sometimes up to 155# and above (body fluids), then back down to 130# a week later – not a constant weight.**

TO NOTE, AS RELATED TO MY HEALTH:

While in Japan 1944-45, on a daily basis to and from work at the steel factory, travel was by train, open flat cars; during bitter cold weather the 18-mile one-way trip for more than 30 minutes was without protective clothing or rain gear. I contracted pneumonia early part of Feb. 1945, with severe chest pains, but I did not run a temp. (fever) & was forced to continue going to the factory; after about a week of this I took the mumps in my left jaw which caused me to be placed in quarantine at the POW Camp – then after about two additional weeks my right jaw began to swell – end result was I spent over 30 days in the camp under quarantine away from the cold train ride, which very likely saved my life.

As far as I know I am the only pneumonia case survivor from the camp. Friends and all those of whom I knew that took pneumonia died about 10 days later while my circumstances resulted in a chronic lung ailment and asthma for the rest of my life.

Please Check Appropriate Square In The Following Table Describing Adequacy Of Diet During Captivity

Average Daily Diet	None	Inadequate	Adequate
Water		**Regularly**	
Broth	X		
Soup With Pieces Of Fish, Meat, Or Poultry		**Maybe once a week able to find a small marble size piece of meat in the soup. Poultry was unheard of.**	
Bread	X	**They don't eat bread regularly.**	
Legumes		**Sometimes in soup – 1 time per week**	
Rice		**The daily diet but not enough**	
Potatoes	X		
Dairy Products	X		
Meat		**About once per wk. – marble size piece if lucky**	
Nuts	X		
Fish		**Grated small fish in water-logged soup – 2 times per wk.**	
Fruits		**About 3 or 4 tangerines at Christmas time**	
Vegetables		**Turnips and radish cooked in watery soup**	
Millet (Small Seeded Cereal and Grasses)	X	**Cereal unheard of – raw weeds picked on camp grounds were eaten.**	

| Other | I often ate raw weeds & leaves of trees – sometimes they were cooked while in the Philippine Islands, also ate the roots of some plants; last 6 months during 1944 while in the Philippines, I ate raw gourd type vegetable on the farm. The prime type vegetables, okra and melons, were for the enemy guards & staff – POWs were limited to leafy vegetables; we were able to steal a cucumber & okra at times and eat it raw. Mainly during 1944, I worked on the farm part-time, other time construction of air landing strip. In the Philippines, mainly 50% of the time I had to rely on edible weeds to get & stay full. |

16. If You Wish, Briefly Describe One Of Your Worst Experiences As A Captive:

Bataan Death March where many were beaten, bayonetted, and shot, sometimes because everyone was weak, drying up of thirst and unable to move – exhaustion, lack of water, food and the tropical heat. It was like I was traveling in a trance, knocked down by one guard, then another, many of us did not have a head covering, driven by heat, thirst at bayonet-point.

17. Specific Diseases Acquired During Captivity: (Answer Yes or No)

Disease	Yes	No	Additional Comments
Dysentery	X		
Malaria	X		
Pneumonia	X		At present it is a chronic recurrent marginal pneumonia 8-10 times per year, has developed into chronic bronchial disease.

Tuberculosis	X		
Worms	X		
Scabies	X		
Skin Disease	X		**Continues at present – have suffered with skin cancers requiring removal and treatment by a dermatologist.**
Vitamin Deficiency Disease	X		
Pellegra	X		**Blisters would come and go.**
Beriberi	X		**Repetitious swellings & excessive body fluids – giving way to aches & pain**
Diphtheria		X	
Other	X		**Dingy Fever – kidney problems & yellow skin**

18. Did You Experience Any Of The Following During Captivity? Answer Yes or No?

Chest Pain **YES** Rapid Heart Beats **YES**

Skipped Or Missed Heart Beats **Unknown** Impaired Vision **YES** Poor Night Vision **YES** Partial Blindness **YES** Eye Ulcers **NO** Hearing Disorder **NO** Bleeding Gums **YES** Toothache **YES** Cavities **1** Tooth Abscess **NO** Loss of Teeth **NO** Sores At The Angles of Mouth **YES** Sore Tongue **YES** Excessive Thirst **X** Swollen Glands **YES** Skin Redness **YES** Blisters **YES** Sunburn **YES** Dry Scaly Skin **YES**

Skin Ulcers **Yes** Boils **No** Pale Skin **YES** Breast Lumps **NO** Nausea **NO** Vomiting **YES** Diarrhea **YES** Episodes Of Jaundice **YES** Chills **YES** Fever **YES** Frequent Urination **YES (10-15 times per night, not less than 4 times)** Bloody Urine **YES** Kidney Stone **NO** Unsteady Gait **YES** Numbness, Tingling Sensation,

Or Pain In The Fingers Or Feet (Electric Foot/Burning Foot) **YES** Numbness Or Weakness In Your Arms And/Or Legs **YES** Aches Or Pains In The Muscles And/Or Joints **YES** Swelling Of The Joints **YES** Swelling Of The Legs And/Or Feet **YES** Swelling Of The Muscles **YES** Fractured Bones **YES** Burns **NO** Psychological Or Emotional Problems **YES (Depression mainly because of weakness & exhaustion, but no worries back home; I was not married.)**

TO NOTE: AS RELATED TO MY VISION (ABOVE):
During the last half of the year 1942 & during the year 1943, I could not recognize a friend or someone I knew more than eight (8) feet away if he did not talk where I could recognize the voice; I could not tell the identities unless about six feet or closer distance.

19. Availability Of Adequate Medical, Surgical, And Dental Treatment During Captivity:

Medical Treatment Was Adequate Yes ____
No **X** **Not even an aspirin for the worst of pain**

If Yes, Describe The Quality
Good ____ Fair ____ Poor **X**

Surgical Treatment Was Adequate
Yes ____ No **X**
I heard of surgeries performed for a few emergencies.

If Yes, Describe The Quality
Good ____ Fair ____ Poor **X**

Dental Treatment Was Adequate Yes No **X**
If Yes, Describe The Quality
Good ____ Fair ____ Poor **X**

Other Operation(s) (Specify) **I saw where a few breasts had been removed from other POWs, they did not wear shirts – I was informed that lumps were removed by American physicians with inadequate equipment with a primitive style set-up (improvised).**

C. History Of Release From Captivity And Repatriation:

1. Date Or Approximate Date Your Captors Lost Control **About August 16, 1945. War ended on 8-15-45.**
2. Date Or Approximate Date You Were Returned to Friendly Control **9-13-45**
3. Briefly Describe The Conditions Of Your Release And Rescue **After news of the Japanese surrender, the camp guards were not in control. They left out because of fear of their war crimes. A couple of my buddies and I finally left the bed-bug infested camp and traveled to the steel mill where we had worked, in the nearby city of Fukuoka, and the nearby sections close to Nagasaki. We eventually split up and I wandered around the Northern sector of Kyshu Island, Japan. I was on my own, so to speak, for about one month. There did not appear to be a government (law-enforcement) in sight. On Sept 10, 1945, I started out hitch-hiking south to Kanoya. The U. S. Forces had just arrived.**
4. In Your Opinion How Thorough Were The Repatriation Examinations? (Including Medical And Psychological Debriefing and Counseling)
   Good ___ Fair ___ Inadequate **X** None **I do not remember any.**
5. Did U.S. Authorities Brief You On The Events Which Occurred While You Were In Captivity? Yes **X** No ___ **Yes, Only one thing, a cowboy singer named Jimmy Davis was elected Governor of Louisiana.**
6. Were You Satisfied With The Way You Were Treated Upon Repatriation? Yes **X** No ___ **There were no restraints; however,**

about 3 months later I wound up in Brooke General Hospital for a longer stay.

7. Were You Given A Disability Rating By The Veterans Administration After Repatriation? Yes X No ___ **After discharge in the year 1949, I received 100% disability rating by the Veterans Administration.**

8. If Yes, What Was The Percentage? Yes X No What Was The Disability? **Malnutrition, incapacitated weakness, asthma, loss of appetite; after returning to American foods, I was very hungry and I began eating about a ½ pound of butter at meal time – then it got to where I could not eat at all – gained more than 50 pounds the first month; some of my friends gained 80 pounds, and others gained 100 pounds the first month. I just could not recognize them afterwards.**

9. Did You Ever Apply To The VA For Dental Care Benefits Based ON Your Former POW Status? Yes X If Yes, Did You Receive A Dental Rating ___ What Was The Rating? **Unknown**

10. Do You Feel That You Were Promoted To The Rank You Would Or Should Have Been If You Had Not Been Captured? Yes No **X According to a letter from a former commanding officer, the late 4-Star General Thomas P. Gerrity, "You should have become at least a M/Sgt. – an honor graduate, Honor Society, doing 4 years of college in 3 ½ years on a walking cane."**

11. Did You Receive The Medals You Believe You Deserved? Yes ___ No X I **received six (6) medals in the year 1983, after more than 40 years per se; now I have written Congressman Huckaby about four (4) others that I have not received.**

D. Adjustment to Post War Life:

1. Did You Continue In Military Service After Rescue? **Yes** If Yes, How Many Additional Years Did You Serve? **2** Did You Perform Reserve Duty? **No** If So, How Many Years? ___

2.	Did You Go To School Following Release From Active Duty? **Yes**
Highest Educational Attainment: **B. S.**
Number Of Years Attended: **3½**

3.	How Soon After Discharge Did You Enter Civilian Employment? **5**
Was This The First Civilian Sector Job You Ever Held? **No**
Did You Return To The Same Job Employed At Prior To Entering Military Service? **No**

4.	Did You Find It Difficult To Adjust To Civilian Life? Yes **?** No
___ My primary weakness was the lack of ability to endure, malnutrition, declining health – a great slowing down process, as opposed to a psychological problem.

5.	How Would You Describe Your Present State Of Health?
Excellent ___ Good ___ Fair ___ Poor **X** Briefly Specify **Very poor, comparatively, if I may describe, back in my earlier days, and particularly after high school, even in school I delighted in working complicated chemistry problems in my head, computing the valences of compounds of three or four steps, also math & geometry. Now it appears that I start out exhausted & end up exhausted. The vibrant energy I once had has disappeared.**

6.	In Spite Of The Many Negative Aspects Of Your POW Status, Were There Any Positive Aspects To Your Experience? Yes **X** No ___
If Yes, Please Specify **Greater faith in God; the greatness of America (U.S.A.); individual courage & dedication is of the utmost importance in the cause of Freedom; never over-react to desperate circumstance, even under hostile captive conditions.**

7.	Please Add Any Additional Comments You Wish.

___

___

___

___

APPENDIX B

Ancillary Articles

Essays from Oriental Slavery

The following letter and four articles are essay-like works I found among my father's writings. I learned in my journey through his writings that he had at one time considered compiling his experiences as individual essays and entitle the work *Essays from Oriental Slavery*.

My dad had shared two of the short essays with me many years before I began the compilation of all his works; others, I had not read. It appears he planned to focus on some of the events and details included in his journaling to create separate accounts of what I believe to be the events salient to him during his experiences on Bataan and in Japan.

For that reason, I have included these as I found them among his writings. ("Leave This World Crying" was not included in his any of his journals and notes.)

Article One: How I Survived

The letter below I did not ever see until I began poring over and organizing my father's folders, <u>and boxes</u>, of his writings written over the years. I do not know the name of the friend to whom he was writing. All I know is that it was dated July 10, 1994.

Dear Friend:

I was not expecting the straightforward question from you at this time as you asked, "How did you get through?" There are two kinds of answers to that question: one is physical and the other is spiritual, and the real answer is "The Good Lord helped me along all the way through." That was for the entire four years.

Back over the years, I often remembered the words of my late grandfather Thomas, who originally came from Pine Bluff, Arkansas. Many times, he often said, "The Bible has all the answers to all of man's problems."

Later on, in years when I was in a difficult situation, with no way out, about to begin a voyage across the Pacific at a time when there was talk of war, I remembered Thomas' sayings. That is when for two days while on Angel Island in

San Francisco Bay, California, I determined to read through my Bible and search for those answers.

By the day we set sail on the SS *President Coolidge*, sailing to our destination under the secret code name "PLUM," I had made a great headway in reading the first few chapters in the book of Genesis. I continued my reading and studying the Scriptures until the last page in the Book of Revelation. This was about six months later while on Bataan in the Philippine Islands.

My Bible became my most prized possession during my time on the Bataan Death March and in the POW camps. I lost it and had it taken from me three times, but it was always returned, as I have shared with you in past days.

Grandfather Thomas, a strong Christian man, was also a wise man. If the leaders of our world today would look to the Bible for the answers to all man's problems, the world would be a happier, more peaceful place.

J C Pardue

Article Two: Leave This World Crying

Attached to this two-page typed composition, which was not a part of the pages and pages of text handwritten by my father over the years, was the following note explaining how he came about the title. He said:

For many years I was put out for a title to one of my most unforgettable episodes of the past, but one morning in the Sunday School assembly, which was being led by Doctor "H," a remark he made gave me the title. He said, "We all come into this world crying." This, I thought, was what I needed for a title, except substitute the first word come to leave, changing the wording of the title to "Leave This World Crying."

Leave This World Crying

There in the shadows was a crying that sounded human. Instantly, I was awakened by the crying voice – awakened to a crying and six words, repeated over and over again, "They can't do this to me! They can't do this to me! I thought for a moment, "How can it be?" The voice was not the voice of an adult and not the voice of a child, but something in between. Fully awakened, finally, I became overshadowed by stark reality: "This place was the Japanese POW Camp, and we were still in Japan."

It was about midnight, and there was cold dreary weather outside the building. The time of the month was mid-February as I remember, and it could have been on Valentine's Day, 1945. I don't remember exactly. At the camp site, three of the twenty buildings were heated during the cold weather. I was just fortunate to be lying on the floor in one of the heated places.

I had been in the isolated section about two weeks. The building was designated as a hospital because it was heated, but still no medicines were to be given to the American POWs. I truly believe the devil (Satan) was the front and leader behind the wicked rationale for this activity. Prior to entering the hospital, I had been working in a Japanese steel factory for around ten days with heavy chest pains from pneumonia; and then I took the mumps in my left jaw. Before being admitted to the hospital, the day-after-day, day-after-day sick calls to see the Japanese doctor had just been wasted effort – until I developed the mumps – and was granted a space on the floor in the hospital building. This night was different from all the others though.

I knew by the cracks in the wall that the continuous crying voice was originating from an isolated, adjacent room. It sounded boyish to me, but there were not supposed to be any babies or children there in the camp. Lying there on the floor surrounded by numerous other mats, my attention was soon drawn to the unusual commotion going on about the place as a result of the crying sounds. People were passing up and down – and back and forth again – through the hallway to the isolated area to investigate the crying.

Lying there on the hospital floor now, a vivid memory permitted a flashback to a time six months earlier in August 1944. I had just finished the 17-day voyage to Japan during which the convoy of ships had encountered two U S submarines; we were hungry and near dehydration from the heat box where we had been shut up in the bottom cargo hole of a Japanese freighter that carried American POWs to Japan, the ships later known as the Japanese Hell Ships. I don't know why that memory appeared in my mind unless the agony I was hearing reminded my subconscious of the agony of that trip,

The darkness seemed to amplify the noises of agony and crying spells of pain as well as the constant distress pleas that went unattended. Through the darkness I crawled to the door leading to the hallway to locate a passer-by and to inquire about the situation of the childlike crying. The information I learned soon spread throughout the camp:

> Initially, the hospital grapevine reported that 'forty American captives, mostly field and staff officers – Army, Navy, Marine, and Air Corp POWs had been brought into the Fukuoka #3 Camp during the night.' Some said, 'These last survivors of several hundred American POWs were picked up when Japanese ships carrying them had been sunk by US planes.' Another source said, 'The two ships the men had been on were sunk – each time after a ship was torpedoed, the floating and living survivors were picked up.'
>
> We learned further, 'These men had made it through on the third ship, but they had been at sea for about three months, and now these last survivors were collapsing. They were ill, starved, and dehydrated. Other facts that came to light was that they had been hastily evacuated from the Philippines as the MacArthur forces began beachhead landings for General Mac's return debut. Some of the officers said that 'only two or three tablespoons of drinking waters were rationed

per man, justified by the rationale that supplies were running low because of the long time that it took in coming through the shipping blockade.'

I heard talk that among the forty survivors was an ill-fated Army colonel, and he was the source of the cries, cries so haunting that they triggered great emotional stress among all who heard them. In fact, the poor soldier became the chief topic in the hospital for the next few dark hours. A close at-hand informant confirmed to me, 'The gasping and crying that you hear so harsh and continuously is from a colonel; he is about dehydrated and he weighs only about seventy pounds."

The intense baby crying spells from the colonel continued to persist in a violent fashion, along with his mingled distress calls and broken speech remarks: "They can't do this to me! They can't do this to me!" Without medication he displayed no verbal or declining tendency of exhaustion until about daybreak when there came a sudden quietness, and I was informed that "after a long duration of heavy crying episodes, a bleak silence and collapse came upon the patient, as the colonel suddenly passed from this world."

With apology, no discourtesy or criticism is meant to the colonel; he was quite obviously in a state of shock at the time, and I might add that was the only crying that I witnessed while a POW in the Far East. About seventy-five percent of the captives who died became motionless and slowly faded away.

Such was the fate of another of the survivors whose silent passing occurred after daylight that morning not far from the colonel's room, in fact, just down the hallway and one door over to the left on the opposite side. I had heard a name that I thought I recognized, so I crawled to see if I might have spent time with him. Since there were no doors to open, I easily crawled on my hands and knees and pulled up by the door facing, standing about four feet in front of a good friend. Lieut. G., who was talking with an American physician. I had worked with the lieutenant on the first day I arrived in Cabanatuan, after the trip from Camp O'Donnell (July of 1942).

Lieut. G. was the mess officer for the rice kitchen. Then in Japan he was one of the few remaining survivors after the long voyage from Philippines Islands. Sitting there on a cabinet top, his feet and legs hanging over the side and with very erect posture, he was telling the physician about some of the hardships that were encountered during the long time at sea. Standing nearby, I thought he could not have weighed more than seventy-five pounds, which is not much muscle AND skin stretched over his six-foot tall body frame. As he sat there without a shirt on, I could count many of his ribs and bones due to his excessive dehydration.

His voice and conversation appeared to be about normal, but he was talking very slowly – a person speaking – moving his mouth – but, otherwise, sitting motionless and frozen as that of a statue. Strangely, as he spoke, he did not move even an eyelid. His eyes were still as if they were fixed in their sockets. I do not think, as close as I was, that he could have seen me. In times past in the Philippines, Lieut. G. was always an alert, close observer with a good sense of humor. On that day, at about 8:00 AM, he was no longer that man. Lieut. G. died later that morning.

The contrast between the deaths of the colonel and Lieut. G. was so striking that I carried the sounds and the sights at the forefront of my mind for many days, and during many nights they haunted me. I did not have the medical knowledge of the physicians in the camps, yet I still found myself attempting to analyze the effect the constant physical pain and eventual emaciation had on their psychological reaction as they faced their impending deaths, one crying loud and long and the other slowly fading away, as I had so often seen.

Article Three: My Trophy of Trophies

My Trophy of Trophies

There is still a mystery about what happened when my bamboo bunk was destroyed many years ago by a dive bomber attack; the known facts make it difficult to sort out the questions and answers. The 17th Bomb Squadron was positioned on the Orion Line of Defense about midway the Bataan Peninsula. We had been there about two months at a time when early one morning a friend and I were roasting peanuts on a small fire at a place about thirty feet away from my elevated bamboo bunk, and we were near the outer shaded edges of a huge mango tree. There were large sprawling branches above us and the trunk of the tree was leaning over near the ground.

Suddenly, there were sounds of an engine cut-out from an enemy dive bomber overhead which meant that it was making a dive to drop the bombs. That sound also meant take cover immediately. For safety, a friend ran and jumped into my foxhole that was about ten feet away; I ran in the opposite direction to get behind the large mango tree. After the bomb exploded, it was not possible for us to recognize the place where we had been seated. From observation the high explosive fragmentation bomb made a bull's-eye target hit on my elevated bed, and a large area was cleared off as if it were a plowed field. All my personal belonging had been destroyed or damaged, and I was most distraught from the loss. More importantly, I felt certain that my Bible no longer existed.

However, in spite of my fears, I went looking for bits of paper from my cherished Bible. I had just recently finished reading through the Holy Bible from Genesis through the Book of Revelation. With many of the verses still fresh and going through mind, I continued to look throughout the entire area. I hoped to find even a few of the pages, tattered or torn. I had always kept the book in a small field bag when I was not reading and studying the verses. Perhaps, I thought, I might find a part of the bag, but I was beginning to doubt I would ever hold my Bible again.

Amazingly, after much searching, I located the bag a distance from the clearing, sitting upright in the underbrush. The Holy Bible was still in the bag just as I had left it − unscathed − but the gold-plated emblem (1941) was not there. The emblem had been fastened on the ring of the zipper chain, and it was not in the bag either. The big question was, and remains to this day, as to how it happened that the emblem was pried loose from the zipper ring and then made to disappear. This was not my primary focus, though, as I now had my Bible back in my possession. And that was the first incident in which I thought for sure my Bible was lost but it was miraculously returned to me.

After the destruction of my elevated bamboo bed, I was forced to move my bivouac to another location where I could sleep on the ground at night, which was necessary after my pup tent and field equipment were obliterated in the bomb explosion. The next day I began to scout and roam north of the Main Defense Line when not on duty watch, just roaming the outer combat zone in search for wild native fruit or anything else edible.

About a week later, during my roaming, I came upon a vacant house which the Filipinos had vacated to get out of the combat zone. Before leaving they had placed their clothing and personal possessions in a shallow above-ground bunker located on one side of the house, but upon looking closer into the entrance of the dugout, I saw that many of the things had been scattered about the outside grounds. When I looked down, my eyes spotted a small girl's hair decoration about half covered with dirt just outside the doorway. The make-up of it consisted of three white doves distinctively represented, but linked together; and there was a metal fastener attached to the back side.

The hair decoration had been trampled in the dust for several days, but it was a beautiful object. As I examined it more closely, I came to the interpretation that the three doves represented the Holy Trinity, and the third dove, which had remained in good condition, was symbolic of the Holy Spirit. Since the house had been vacated, possibly never to be occupied again, and there was no one left to protect things in the combat zone, I detached the last dove with my pocket knife and carried it back with me to the bivouac area. I then drilled a small hole through one of the dove's wings and immediately located the small dove on the ring of my Bible zipper chain. The Bible with the dove that was so symbolic to me would travel with me on the Bataan Death March, tied up with a strap, allowing it to swing from the strap looped around my neck.

On the day that we departed the Philippines for Japan two and one-half years later, the Bible was taken from me and thrown about thirty (30) feet below to the bottom hold of the Hell Ship, *Nissyo Maru*. At that moment I thought for sure that it was the last of my Holy Bible. One week later, a stranger evaded the security and went below and started scavenging through the large piles of junk that had been thrown in the hold looking for something to eat. Amazingly, he found my Bible in the darkness, brought it up to our cargo hold and began searching for the owner. The captives were sitting, crowded elbow to elbow, on the compartment floor when I saw someone within the group reach out and hand me the Bible. I sensed it with such a strong feeling that it was almost as if I had just taken a shot in the arm. Then I once again remembered seeing is believing. And this was the third time my Bible was miraculously returned to me.

Article Four: The Lowest Point

The Lowest Point

An official once asked me, "What do you remember as your lowest point of let-down or depression during the four-year Pacific War (1941-1945)?"

I said, "Vividly, for me, one incident: walking on the bodies of dead people in the dark has always stayed well hidden, way back in my mind, when on August 8, 1945 – a time at the steel factories – just east of Nagasaki, Japan, when the second A-bomb was dropped.

We arrived that morning and just waited around – waiting for something to happen. Two days earlier, American B-29 Bombers flew over our area on the Northern Kyshu Island and dropped aerial leaflets that warned the steel factory would be bombed on August 8.

At 12:00 noon the heavy bombardment started and continued until about 4:00 PM that day with many types of bombs. Some of them made the surroundings shake like that of an earthquake, and there were many cluster fire bombs dropped throughout the region. It was dark outside because of the heavy black smoke.

After the bombing stopped, the officials said, "All Clear!" Then the American POWs were advised to hike to the train station about a mile away for the electric train ride to camp, which was about a twenty-mile journey. When we arrived at the station, someone said, "No electricity, so you'll have to wait about an hour or longer for a steam engine train."

At that moment, I realized that I had left the factory and left my canteen water bottle at the Ichi Seiko plant. Immediately, without a word, I turned around and started running back to the steel factory. There were no lights anywhere to see the way back to the factory building, and the exceedingly large clouds of black smoke consumed the space. Although I could make out the large buildings from their outline in the sky, which, fortunately, provided me the direction to travel, the roadway was not visible. The atmosphere was darker than night.

When I arrived at the factory and went running around the corner, still about seventy-five feet from the building, I ran over something and fell over it – on to something else – bodies of dead people. There were so many of them. I got up running and fell again. Then, I realized that the bodies were the bodies of the Korean slave women, one after another, sprawled everywhere. After that realization, I started working my way over and around the dead bodies on my way to the factory entrance. When I located my water canteen in the thick darkness of the dungeon, I turned around, then again started working my way back through the darkness and around the dead bodies that covered the street. Somewhat numb and sickened, I began once again on my journey to the train station.

We learned later that the slave women had been housed in an open warehouse during the bombardment, and all of them died there. When the bombing stopped and the American POW slaves left for the train station, the Nipponese (Japanese) factory workers then dragged the dead bodies outside and left them in the street.

Article Five: Ruminations on Hara Kari

Ruminations on *Hara-Kari* (Hari Kari)

The Japanese soldiers and guards considered those who surrendered to be cowards. According to their Bushido Code, instead of surrendering to the enemy, a soldier should commit *hara kari* (also called *hari-kiri* and/or spelled *harakiri*), which is the Japanese ritual suicide by disembowelment. Therefore, the Japanese considered the Americans to be cowards in spite of the fact that the soldiers on Bataan "were surrendered" by their leaders. They actually had nothing to do with the decision. This did not make any difference to the Japanese. As a result, many of the Japanese guards encouraged POWs to commit *hari kari*.

As a POW on Bataan and in Japan, I was told by guards that I should commit *hara kari*. Of course, I never considered it, and I never knew anyone who gave in to the guards' harassment to execute the Japanese ritual suicide. I did, however, watch some POWs who were unable to cope give up and seem to accept their impending death, which some might consider another means of killing oneself. About a week after the Bataan Death March when we had made it to Camp O'Donnell, I saw this happen as I watched a friend that I had known for years give up his life. An intelligent gentleman, he was clean cut and polite. It was the first case I witnessed and most disturbing to watch, I think, because there was not anything I could do to prevent it.

"Are you eating the rice, M.," I asked.

I received no reply. His mind was not there as he sat gazing into space. He had given up the desire for a forceful determination to eat the small amount of rice he received. He preferred just to sit and to stare into space with a blank expression on his face. I wondered if his mind was back in the states with his wife. Many of the young soldiers were newlyweds. Perhaps, I thought, he was dreaming of sitting before a table of finely cooked American foods, purging his mind of any desire to eat the starvation rice diet. Whatever was in his mind, he had abandoned not only everyone surrounding him but also himself.

A captive of his own imagination, he, like some of the others trapped by this misery, died within twenty-four hours of the time he gave in to the lack of a will to live. That despondency was a powerful force. I thought a lot about the morbid despondency which took over my friend's life, and I wondered if this could be considered a sublimated type of suicide. I questioned what could be behind this spirit that would cause an individual to give up his will to live. Is there any relationship between the soldier who is persuaded to end his life in violent disaster and the one who is not willing to face horrors because he concludes there is no hope left? What brings about the feeling that the odds are too great?

My first thought was the physical aspect. Was it the total exhaustion and the dehydration we were all suffering as a result of the lack of ample water and food during and after the Death March? Although the effect of physical weakness was a huge consideration, I contemplated also that the change from a well, sound moderate manner of living to that of a "pig in a pen" might be even more likely and disastrous. Like all the others, I am sure, I never expected to be starved to death, not to mention the tortures, brutalities, and the constant presence of death.

Or was this rejection of life a result of the mental defeat after the military capitulation? In the eyes of some, we had failed. However, we had given it our all, I thought. I had seen firsthand my fellow soldiers continuing to fight when they knew—we all knew—a defeat was inevitable. Still, I could not imagine giving in to the despondency overcoming many of the prisoners. This bothered me even after returning home safely myself. I was saddened when I remembered soldier friends who succumbed to a lack of willingness to live.

After study and contemplation through the years, it appeared to me that the answer might possibly be found within each individual's constitution, what I call the genetic make-up with which we are all born. Those are the genes that give us our physical traits, temperament, personality, character, to name a few. Then the environment to which we are exposed must be factored into the mix. I am not presuming to be a psychology expert, but these ideas surely hold the key to understanding why two soldiers with similar characteristics and background who are suffering the same horrific conditions respond so differently. One possesses the ability to "will" himself to live and the other gives up.

I thought about this for a long time after I returned from the Philippines. Watching friends die from brutality and torture became a part of all our lives, but what troubled me most was the soldier friend who, for some reason, reached a point some might call the point of no return—refusing food, staring into space with that mindless gaze, oblivious to others—where there's no turning back—and then giving in to death.

Life was too precious to me to consider giving it up, even when I was exhausted, hungry, dehydrated, and in pain. I did not want to give the sadistic, ruthless guards the pleasure of thinking they had pressured me into hari-kari or any other type of suicide. I never reached that point of no return. Despite the barbarians and our barbaric surroundings, I wanted to stay alive and return home to my family. And I did—with my Bible in hand and my Lord in my heart—I returned to my homeland with a faith and a love of life and my God that I did not possess when I boarded the USS *Coolidge* in 1941. The psychologists may one day uncover deeper meanings surrounding "the will to live," but in my case, my faith was the source of my strength. I know this to be true.

Front page of *Los Angeles Examiner* on Friday, January 28, 1944, after the government finally allowed release of reports of conditions on Bataan Death March and in POW camps. The news horrified the nation and was followed by a public outcry for action.

Official Military Photograph of Private J.C. Pardue
after enlistment in the Army Air Corps in 1939

Private J.C. Pardue on Barksdale   Photo on Hunter Field, in
Air Force Base, Bossier City,   Savannah, Georgia, labeled
Louisiana, in 1939, in front   on back of photo as "J. C.
of an A-18 attack plane   Pardue and His Crew." Private
                                          Pardue on far right of photo

My father's treasured Bible, which survived a direct hit from a fragmentation bomb, confiscation at Camp O'Donnell, and the voyage on the Hell Ship *Nissyo Maru*.

The spine of the Bible indicates its delicate condition as a result of the time spent in the Philippines. It came home, however, with my father.

After the Bible was taken from my father in the prison camp, it was screened before it was returned to him with the Japanese stamp of approval.

My father wrote about finding the white dove at an abandoned Filipino house and attaching it to his Bible.

The SS *President Coolidge*

The SS *President Coolidge*, completed in 1931, was one of the luxury ocean liners transformed into a troopship to transport soldiers from the United States to the Far East during World War II. The 27th Bombardment Group traveled from San Francisco, California, to Manila, in the Philippine Islands, in November of 1941, offering soldier boys like my father a look at luxury travel on the Pacific. The SS *Coolidge* served the military from late in 1941 until October 25, 1942 when she hit a mine and sank near the New Hebrides.

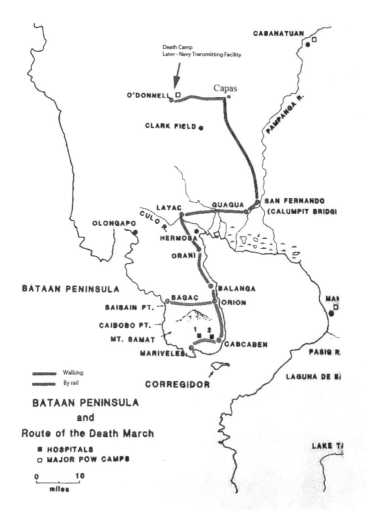

The Bataan Death March began at the tip of the Bataan Peninsula where the American and Filipino soldiers were told to go after General King surrendered them. They were force-marched approximately sixty-five miles from Mariveles to San Fernando where they were loaded into train boxcars to Capas. They were then marched approximately eight to nine miles to Camp O'Donnell, one of the most heinous of the POW camps. Some captives who did not begin at Mariveles, but who joined the march later, did not march the total route.

The March of Death

National Archives

This photograph portrays a large group of POWs, but not all the prisoners were marched in large groups like this one. This photograph was very likely used for Japanese propaganda. Some POWs were in columns of two and spaced more widely apart, especially as the days passed and many fell, too exhausted to continue. They had begun the march weak and exhausted after fighting almost four months without adequate food, with many suffering from the jungle diseases. If they fell, they were bayonetted, shot, or buried alive. The *Los Angeles Examiner* used this same photograph on their paper's front page the day the horrors of Bataan were exposed to the nation.

The Japanese "Sun Treatment"

Photograph of my father, J.C. Pardue, and several of his 27th Bomb Group friends enduring the infamous Japanese "sun treatment." After a few hours marching north on the first day, around 11:00 a.m., my father noted that "[they] were instructed to move off the road and bunch up close together in the open 100-degree sunshine [and to] remove all head coverings." My dad had identified himself and several of his friends, but I removed the names. His profile can be seen at the top of the picture, above the last set of clasped hands.

Diagram of Camp Cabantuan

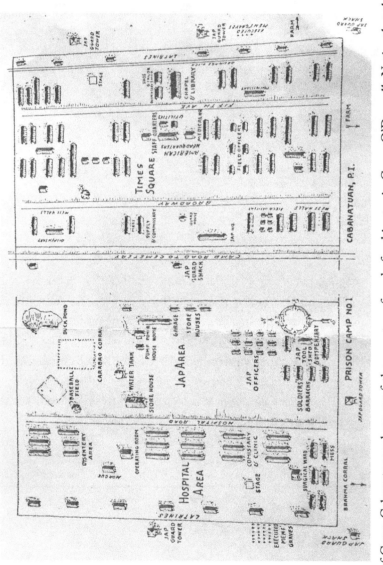

Diagram of Camp Cabanatuan where my father was transferred after his stay in Camp O'Donnell. Notice that the POWs labeled one area "Times Square," not that it was anything like Times Square.

Camp Fukuoka #3 in Japan

A photograph in my father's files, which was labeled on the back in his handwriting "Fukuoka #3 POW Camp, Japan, Island of Kyshu, Taken 9-13-1945." According to his journals and letters, it was one of several photographs sent to him by Ben H. Williams, a War Crimes Investigator.

Letters from—and to—Home

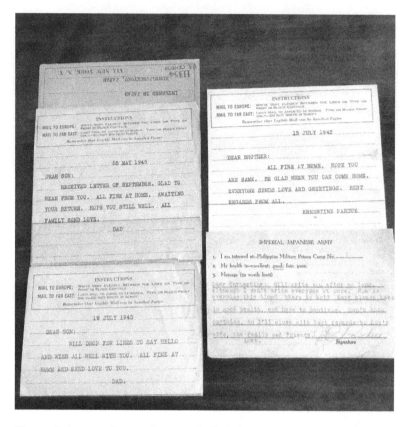

Pictured above are letters from my dad's father and sister as well as a letter my dad wrote from camp to his sister. All letters were limited to a certain number of words and were screened before mailing.

Letter of Appreciation

Dear Corporal Pardue:

General Arnold has asked me to send you the following message: "It was with a great deal of personal pleasure that I learned of your return to the Air Forces. We are proud of what you did and thankful for your safe return. Welcome back. Arnold."

As for myself, I cannot praise too highly the courage and fortitude which you have displayed in the face of extraordinary hardships throughout the time you were a prisoner of war. Your faith and loyalty have been a real contribution to victory.

I want to congratulate you on the way you have upheld the dignity and prestige of our country under the most trying conditions and to join General Arnold in welcoming you back.

Sincerely,

GEORGE C. KENNEY,
General, United States Army,
Commanding.

Cpl. J. C. Pardue,
Marion, Louisiana

The **Letter from General George C. Kenney,** which my father received after his reenlistment on August 8, 1946, expresses both his own and General Hap Arnold's gratitude for his service as well as their appreciation that he had reenlisted for three more years.

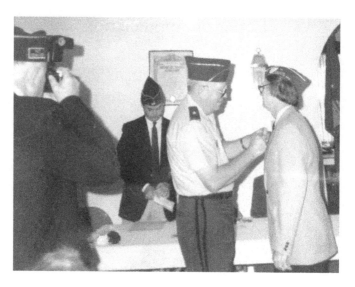

A Veteran of Foreign Wars ceremony in Monroe, Louisiana, to honor those who had served and suffered for freedom.

XPOW J. C. Pardue with his granddaughter, Amy Hill (Amy Hill Bourgeois), who was allowed to miss school to view a ceremony honoring her grandfather.

The Bronze Star Medal

J. C. Pardue was awarded the Bronze Star medal in a ceremony on September 28, 1984, onBarksdale Air Force Base. He was among sixteen other Louisiana members of the World War II27th Bombardment Group who were honored with the award almost forty years after the end of the war.

THE UNITED STATES OF AMERICA

TO ALL WHO SHALL SEE THESE PRESENTS, GREETING:

THIS IS TO CERTIFY THAT
THE PRESIDENT OF THE UNITED STATES OF AMERICA
AUTHORIZED BY EXECUTIVE ORDER, AUGUST 24, 1962
HAS AWARDED

THE BRONZE STAR MEDAL

TO

Sergeant J. C. Pardue

FOR

Meritorious Achievement
20 November 1941 to 11 September 1945

GIVEN UNDER MY HAND IN THE CITY OF WASHINGTON
THIS   3d   DAY OF   May   19 84

CHIEF OF STAFF

SECRETARY OF THE AIR FORCE

XPOW J. C. Pardue received the Bronze Star in a ceremony on Barksdale Air Force Base, forty-five years after he enlisted there in 1939. It took many years for former POWs to receive the medals they had earned on the Bataan Death March, in the POW camps, and as slaves in Japan.

The Purple Heart—at Last

On October 6, 2003, J.C. Pardue received the Purple Heart from Congressman Rodney Alexander, who supported and facilitated documentation of the award after the doctor who had treated my father had been burned alive in the POW camp. Pictured also is my mother, Demaris Pardue.

Photograph of the *Bataan (LHD 5)*, the United States Navy multipurpose amphibious assault ship named in honor of the soldiers who served on the Bataan Peninsula. Bataan survivors and their guests were honored on this massive ship in Pascagoula, Mississippi, on May 18, 1996.

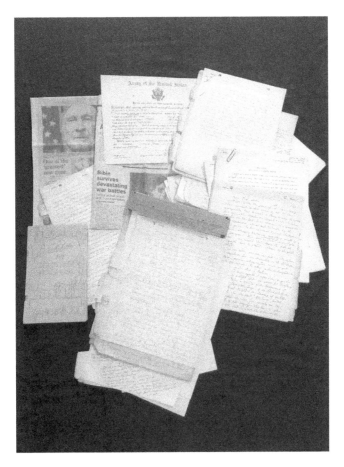

Some of the <u>many</u> pages of my father's journaling and rough drafts, both handwritten and typed, of his experiences from his enlistment and training to his return to America, including the Bataan Death March, in POW camps, and as a slave in the Japanese steel factory. As I pored over those aged journals and essays, written so long ago with the edges flaking away on some of them, it seemed at times my dad was talking to me as I compiled his stories. Notice the booklet (on the far left), entitled "Orientation for Recovered Personnel," which my father received at the 29th Repatriation Depot in Manila in 1945. It is falling to pieces, but still intact—my dad saved everything!

Medals Earned in the Fight for Country

My father proudly displayed the medals awarded to the United States Army
Air Corps 27th Bomb Squad during World War II. He was most proud
of the Bronze Star and the Purple Heart (from the left side, the first and
second medals on the top row).

NOTES

1   Pardue, interview by Janis Pardue Hill, Monroe, LA, July 21, 2010–June 8, 2012. In compiler/editor's possession.

2   Pardue, personal documents, 1951-2008. In compiler/editor's possession.

3   D'Estes, *Eisenhower: A Soldier's Life*, 277.

4   Milton, "Area Survivors of Bataan Death March Tell of Ordeals. *Monroe Morning World*, 4B.

5   Manchester, *American Caesar: Douglas MacArthur 1880-1964*, 311.

6   "Bataan Wounded Lived with Pain." *Life*, 33.

7   Simonton, "Time of Suffering." Sunday Feature Article. *Monroe Morning World*. 1B.

8   McCoy, Mellnik, and Kelley, "Death Was Part of Our Life: How 5200 Americans and Thousands of Filipinos Died in Jap Prison Camps." *Life*, 28-29.

9   Dyess, *Bataan Death March: A Survivor's Account*, 25.

10 Manchester, *American Caesar: Douglas MacArthur 1880*-1964, 269.

11 *Ibid*.

12 *Ibid*, 452.

13 Martin and Stephenson, *Operation PLUM: The Ill-Fated 27th Bombardment Group and the Fight for the Western Pacific*, 289.

14 *Ibid*, 289-290.

15 Evans, Robbie. "Symbol of Sacrifice: World War II Vet, POW Awarded Purple Heart." 1A.

16 United State Navy, *Bataan (LHD 5): United States Navy Multipurpose Amphibious Assault Ship*, 1.

17 *Ibid*, 4.

18 *Ibid*.

19 Rogers, "One of the 'Greatest' Now Gone." *The News Star*, 8A.

20 *Ibid*.

21 Orwell, *1984*, i.

BIBLIOGRAPHY

"Bataan Wounded Lived with Pain." *Life*. April 20. 1942. 32-35.

D'Este, Carlo. *Eisenhower: A Soldier's Life*. New York: Henry Holt, 2003.

Dyess, William E. *Bataan Death March: A Survivor's Account*. Lincoln, NE: University of Nebraska Press, 1944.

Evans, Robbie. "Symbol of Sacrifice: World War II Vet, POW Awarded Purple Heart." *The News Star. October* 7, 2003. 1A, 8A.

Manchester, William. *American Caesar: Douglas MacArthur 1880-1964*. New York: Dell, 1979.

Martin, Adrian R, and Larry W. Stephenson. *Operation Plum: The Ill-Fated 27th Bombardment Group and the Fight for the Western Pacific*. College Station: Texas A&M Press, 2008.

McCoy, Melvyn, S.M. Mellnik, and Welbourn Kelley. "Death Was Part of Our Life: How 5200 Americans and Thousands of Filipinos Died in Jap Prison Camps." *Life*. Feb. 7, 1944. 26-31, 96-98, 100, 102, 105-106, 108, 111.

Milton, Bill. "Area Survivors of Bataan Death March Tell of Ordeals." *Monroe Morning World. April* 9, 1967. 4B.

Orwell, George. *1984*. United Kingdom: Penguin Publishing Group, 1950.

Pardue, J.C. Interviews by Janis Pardue Hill. July 21, 2010– June 8, 2012.

Pardue, J.C. Personal Documents. 1951-2008.

Rogers, Scott. "One of the 'Greatest' Now Gone." *The News Star.* June 30, 2012. 1A.

Roosevelt, Franklin D. *Declaration of War Speech*. Congress. Washington, D.C.: Government Printing Office, December 8, 1941.

Simonton, Robert. "Time of Suffering." Sunday Feature Article. *Monroe Morning World.* July 25, 1965. 1B.

United States Infantry Association. "Japanese Manifesto." *Infantry Journal: Overseas Edition. The War in the Pacific.* Washington, D.C.: Infantry Journal, Inc., Aug. 1944.

United States Navy. *Bataan (LHD 5): United States Navy Multipurpose Amphibious Assault Ship*. Official Program for the Christening of the *Bataan (LHD 5)*. Pascagoula, MS: Litton Industries, 1996.

ABOUT THE COMPILER/ EDITOR

Dr. Janis Pardue Hill, a retired professor from Louisiana Tech University, has spent forty years in Louisiana education in various roles: secondary classroom teacher, curriculum coordinator, program coordinator at the Louisiana Department of Education (DOE), curriculum consultant, and university professor. Although she loved the university, her colleagues and her students, both undergraduate and graduate, she will quickly confess that her heart rests in the high school classroom where she used literature to teach reading and writing skills, critical thinking skills, and above all, the desire to be a lifelong learner. Dr. Hill holds a BS in Health, Physical and Safety Education with a minor in English; an MA in English; and a PhD in Curriculum Theory with an emphasis on English.

Besides teaching, Dr. Hill also served on innumerable Department of Education committees during the development of the Louisiana English Language Arts (ELA) Standards as well as the state ELA high standards tests at the eighth and tenth grade levels. She also worked on the development of the ELA Grade Level Expectations (GLEs) for the Louisiana DOE and in 2003 authored the *Louisiana Model Curriculum* for the English Language Arts Grade-Level Activities (Grades 9-12). As a Program Coordinator at the DOE, she recruited and worked with classroom teachers on the SAGE (Supporting Academic Growth in Education) project. Always an advocate for the inclusion of teachers in the curriculum development and testing process, Dr. Hill served as a consultant for several parishes in Louisiana, working with state classroom teachers on the development of local standards and curriculum.

Dr. Hill retired to dedicate herself to family, with the publication of her father's notes and journals her top priority. She spent the last two years of her father's life talking with and interviewing him, years she will quickly affirm remain as some of the most joyful times in her life. Determined to finish the work to honor her father and the other courageous defenders of Bataan, Dr. Hill believes fervently that *these stories must be shared with the children and grandchildren of "The Greatest Generation" and that each of their stories is an integral part of their collective history as well as the history of the American people.*

Dr. Hill has been married for fifty-two years to her childhood sweetheart, Charles A. Hill, Jr., a career law enforcement agent;

and they are the parents of two children, Trey Hill and Amy Hill Bourgeois, and grandparents of three grandchildren, Jack Hill, Harper Bourgeois, and Emma Bourgeois. They now reside on Lake Claiborne in North Louisiana.